A Pub On Every Corner

Volume Three: North Liverpool

Freddy O'Connor

The Bluecoat Press

©1998 Freddy O'Connor

Published by
Bluecoat Press
Liverpool

Book design by
March Design
Liverpool

Printed by
Design2Print
Llandudno

Front cover: Beer house, Athol Street - coloured by Will Curwin
Back cover: Black Bull, Aintree - coloured by Peter Turner

ISBN 1 872568 57 2

To my wife, Jean, for her help and support and to my father.

Acknowledgments
The author is grateful for the assistance given by: The management of the Chaser, Longmoor Lane, Fazakerley and the Linacre Hotel, Linacre Lane, Bootle.
Frank Duggan, Roger Hull, Steve Lightwater, Bryn Jones, Eddie Murphy (Great Howard Street area) Dominic Whelan (Commercial Road and Stanley Road areas) and Ted Williams.
Liverpool Records Office
Crosby Library
City Engineer's Department
Tetley Walker (Estates Department)
Walton-On-The-Hill History Group

Special thanks to John McKeown, for invaluable research, material and photographs.

Pubs 'not listed' in any given era mean the premises were closed, but may have reopened either as a pub, or another business at a later date, whereas pubs listed 1964 or 1970 were all open in those years, but have since closed or been demolished. Modern pubs, unless relevant to the text, have been omitted.

Abbreviations used in this publication are as follows:

BH	BEER HOUSE
PH	PUBLIC HOUSE
SD	SPIRIT DEALER
SV	SPIRIT VAULTS
WSD	WINE & SPIRIT DEALER
WSM	WINE & SPIRIT MERCHANT
WSV	WINE & SPIRIT VAULTS

Introduction

Over the years, beer houses had various licenses. Some were only able to serve selected drinks on the premises, whilst others could sell selected drinks to take off the premises. Grocer shops were often licensed as beer houses and many were the forerunners of today's off licenses. For the purpose of this publication, I am therefore classing them all simply as beer houses (BH).

Numerous BHs and SVs in Liverpool originated from an Act of 1830, which enabled any ratepayer to acquire a beer license for two guineas. This misguided Act was a continuation of earlier failed policies. As long ago as 1495, it was recognised that there were already too many ale houses in the country and the first Licensing Act of 1552 observed that:

'For as much as intolerable hurts and troubles to the commonwealth of this realm do daily grow and increase through such abuses and disorders as are had and used in common alehouses and other houses called tippling houses; and on grounds of public policy, the justices were empowered to remove, discharge and put away the common selling of ale and beer in such towns or places where they shall think and meet.'

Despite various Acts, the level of drunkenness steadily increased and, by the time of James 1, punishment was severe. Fines were imposed on the poor and those who could not pay were put in the stocks (surprisingly this punishment was in use as late as 1872). An Act passed on the accession of Charles 1 (1625) for permitting 'tippling', was extended to ale-house keepers, innkeepers, vinters and victuallers. Anyone found without a license was to forfeit 21/- or, if in default, to be whipped. A second offence was punishable by a month in the House of Correction.

Although malt liquor had been the main drink of the masses since the 17th Century, the drinking of spirits gradually became more common. The outbreak of Civil War in 1643 was to fundamentally change drinking habits, with the introduction of taxation.

In order to increase the National Revenue, excise duty was imposed on ale, beer, cider and perry. Once implemented, more increases followed. For example, tax was 2/6d on a barrel of beer in 1650, rising to 5/- a barrel by 1692. The tax on beer in 1692, led to the widespread consumption of alternative drinks, particularly gin, leading to widespread drunkenness and lawlessness throughout the 18th century. Such was the rapid and widespread consumption of gin that it became known as 'gin fever'. Gin and grog shops sprang up everywhere and it is reckoned that in London alone, over 7000 existed by the early 1720s. (Compared with the insignificant number from the following report; 'in the reign of Edward III (1327-1377) only three taverns were allowed in London: one in Chepe, one in Walbrook and the other in Lombard Street.')

To stem the tide of drunkenness that was sweeping the country, an alarmed Government slapped a 20/- increase on tax and, in 1736, compelled retailers to pay £50 for a license. Resentment to this huge increase led to widespread 'gin riots' and such was the massive, illicit trading in gin, the Act was a complete failure. Distillers, for example, took out wine licenses whilst selling a concoction of gin, sugars and spices as wine, and taverns and pubs simply sold gin under a variety of names. Drunkenness in the 18th century was not confined to the so-called 'lower classes'. Such was the acceptance of excessive drinking that the vice was common to rich and poor alike. At social gatherings, for example, a gentleman would never leave a table sober. In fact, it would have been considered an insult to his host if he did. The failure of the government to halt excessive gin drinking continued until 1828, when a new Act was brought out with the intention of restoring the ancient popularity of beer in favour of spirits. A further Act in 1830 extended this trend.

The emphasis had shifted but the problem continued as beer houses (BHs) replaced gin shops and various Acts were brought out throughout the 19th century to combat the 'demon drink'.

Although drunkeness was still a problem, particularly in the slums that were associated with the early, basic one roomed or cellar beer houses, it never reached the pinnacle of a century earlier. (When the 1830 Act came out, some 50 licenses a day for BHs were issued for several weeks in Liverpool alone). By the 1840s, over 900 BHs were trading in the town alongside nearly 1500 PHs.

The early years of the 20th century brought a rapid and sharp decline of the numerous licensed premises (particularly BHs), through an act of 1904, whilst the final demise of BHs is still within living memory.

Just before the outbreak of the First World War, the number of licensed premises in Liverpool were as follows:

Public Houses	1453
Beer Houses	119
Refreshment Houses (licensed)	212
Grocers (licensed) and Off Licenses	146

This gives a total number of 1930 licensed premises (discounting clubs) which, although a huge amount, was over 500 less than some 50 years earlier.

North Liverpool

The north end of Liverpool, with four major thoroughfares running north from the city centre, once contained an incredible number of licensed houses: Dock Road (starting at Goree/Strand), approximately 105; Great Howard Street, approximately 60; Vauxhall Road, approximately 75; Scotland Road, approximately 110. (These figures do not include previous names of pubs listed). The majority of these pubs are, in the main, beyond living memory.

Prior to the 1820s, few pubs existed, thereafter they became abundant as the population and slum property dramatically increased. Prospering for some 50 years, they began to decline as the slums were cleared and industrial premises and the railway took over large tracts of land. The highest number of licensed

houses, which existed amongst some 3000 courts, occurred in the mid-nineteenth century. This figure reduced to 1510 by 1895, in line with the downturn of licensed premises. The decline set in more rapidly in the middle years of the twentieth century, when war damage and the subsequent demolition of the central areas of the city from the 1950s onwards cleared numerous pubs. The old corner locals are still continuing to close to the present day albeit at a slower rate.

For the purpose of this publication, the first three thoroughfares and vicinity are featured under the title Vauxhall. Other areas covered are: Kirkdale, Walton, Bootle and selected districts on the northern outskirts of the city.

Vauxhall

The north Dock Road and surrounds, from the Pier Head vicinity through to the Gladstone Dock, have altered enormously in recent years as the older docks are no longer used for their original purpose. The far north docks are still a hive of activity but, because of modern technology, most ships are in and out of the port within a day or two.

Before the 1970s, the whole area was crammed with dock related industries and during the 1950s and earlier, the mean, crowded streets off the Dock Road housed thousands of dockers and dock related workers in squalor, just a stones throw from their place of work.

On the west side of the Dock Road, there are no pubs. Before the great docks were constructed, the 'north shore' was a pleasant seaside retreat containing a number of old inns. This was a very different environment to the public houses built later on the east side of the road. Vandries House was an ancient inn owned by a Dutchman named Vandries, whose name is perpetuated in a street off the Dock Road – Vandries Street, close to the site of the old inn. Vandries House was also named the Grapes Inn and the North Shore Coffee House. The premises were demolished by the early 1840s.

Other inns of the north shore included Bowling Green Inn, Mile End House and the Horse and Jockey. All these inns were cleared as the docks were extended northwards from the early 19th century.

Although often referred to as the Dock Road, the name does not actually exist. A succession of names northward from the Pier Head are as follows: Goree/The Strand (L2), Georges Dock Gates (L3), New Quay (L3), Bath Street (L3), Waterloo Road (L3) and Regent Road (L3, L5 and L20). A greatly reduced number of pubs still remain on the Dock Road's east side. The following were/are on the Dock Road:

Goree Piazzas/Liverpool Arms

The name Goree Piazzas was given to two magnificent blocks of warehouses, shown in the photograph above, which separated Goree (West) from Back Goree (later named the Strand) and now a widened thoroughfare that sweeps past the Pier Head (although still named Goree and The Strand). This unusual name was taken from a bare rock, off Cape Verde, where slaves were kept prior to shipment to the plantations. This view from 1913 features the demolition of warehouses on Back Goree, south of Water Street.

The Liverpool Arms, partially hidden behind a tram, displays the words 'Threlfalls Liverpool and Salford Ales'. The premises was listed at 27-29 Water Street and had two entrances in Water Street, two in Back Goree and two in Goree Piazzas. The original building was listed at 28 Water Street at the junction of Stringers Alley. A peculiarity of this pub was the fact that the locals mostly drank whisky, day and night, from teapots amidst shouts of 'more tea', 'fill 'em up' and 'fill the pot'. The reason why this curious eccentricity took place is unknown. Maybe it started as a joke that caught on and became a tradition within the pub.

Generations of drinkers have always claimed that beer and spirits were stronger during their day and older people reading this publication may agree with this statement when comparing alcohol today to what they supped during their younger days. Customers who frequented the old Liverpool Arms over a hundred years ago and drank their whisky from black and brown earthenware teapots, would no doubt drink today's generation under the table!

The Goree warehouses, originally containing two other pubs, were built in 1793 and rebuilt in 1802 after a disastrous fire. Sadly, although surviving war damage, these magnificent old warehouses finally met their fate to the bulldozer in 1957.

When the topic of slavery comes up, the warehouses are regularly referred to with stories of slaves being shackled in the open arcade of the Goree warehouses. This has never been ascertained and is probably a myth (although there is no smoke without fire and what may have fuelled such stories is that earlier warehouses did exist before the Goree).

A large part of the city's wealth was made from fortunes through 'privateering' and slave trading. Up to the early years of the 19th century, they were quite legitimate branches of business. A man in command of a slave ship, for example, may have studied for and entered the ministry and nobody would have thought it unusual. Slave dealing was as much accepted as any other means of making a living and few people ventured to dispute the trade.

Documentation proved that slaves were sold in Liverpool, although the actual number would have been negligible compared to the huge numbers shipped directly from Africa to the Americas. This cruel trade took many years to eradicate and, right up to abolition, the town's merchants, the Corporation and wealthy ship owners in particular, were still firmly against ending slavery, claiming that it would ruin the town. This, of course, was to be the reverse after its abolition.

The main instigator for abolition was the great reformer William Wilberforce (1759-1833). By 1807, the trade was prohibited, although total abolition did not occur through out the British Empire until 1833, ironically just after Wilberforce's death.

As an insight, in 1802, 30796 slaves were carried by Liverpool ships, dropping to 15534 in 1803, although an upsurge occurred in the final fifteen months to 1807, with 185 Liverpool ships engaged in the trade, carrying 43755 slaves.

Privateering (where armed vessels were owned and officered by private persons holding commissions from the Government that gave them the authority to fire against hostile nations, especially in capture of merchant shipping) was as cruel as slave trading, but when a ship returned to the town with a captured ship, the bloodshed that usually occurred with the capture was not of the slightest interest to anyone. The rewards, like slave dealing, were enormous although the perils of the sea were always a hazard in both trades.

One example occurred in 1756, when a Liverpool vessel St George, carrying 12 guns and 80 men and commanded by Fortunatus Wright, was in the port of Leghorn (Livorno) Italy when a large French xebec, carrying 16 guns and about 160 men, fixed her position at the harbour in order to intercept British commerce. Wright weighed anchor, hoisted sail and engaged the xebec. He overcame the enemy and returned to the harbour in triumph with the captured vessel (the French captain, lieutenant and some sixty men were killed). During the voyage home to England, Wright's vessel foundered and all on board perished.

One of the most notable slave traders was John Newton (1725-1807) who was in command of a slave ship whilst studying for the ministry. He was later to join the movement to abolish slavery, assisting William Wilberforce. He eventually became a clergyman and a noted hymn writer, his most famous composition being the renowned 'Amazing Grace'.

Northward from Goree/The Strand is George's Dock Gates (no pubs listed), then New Quay, which contained 15 public houses on its length of 219 yards (four in the 1820's), which, together with all the following pubs along the North Dock Road, were all located on its eastern side.

Princes and British Queen

The photograph (opposite top) from the late 1920s features two of the pubs of New Quay, the Princes and the British Queen. The Princes was listed at the junction of Chapel Street and prior to the 1860s, had the unusual name of Number Four (an earlier building). The Atlantic Tower hotel now occupies the site.

The British Queen, the building next but one was, pre-1860s, listed as the British Queen and Eating House. As a result of the construction of the Dock Road branch of the first Mersey Tunnel, they were both demolished in 1930. The warehouses further along New Quay survived until the early 1970s.

The continuation of New Quay is Bath Street, named after the

former sea-water baths that were located here until 1817, before demolition began for the building of Princes Dock.

The street contained some 12 public houses on its length of 347 yards. With the ever increasing trade of the last century, most of the pubs of Bath Street were cleared to make way for the construction of warehouses. Only one survived until the 1960s, the Old Fort Hotel at the junction of Dennison Street, so named after a former fort and barracks that were located facing the street and later cleared for the construction of the Princes Dock.

The continuation of Bath Street is Waterloo Road, which along its frontage still contains some old property. It once contained some 37 public houses along its length of 810 yards. The following were/are on Waterloo Road:

Princes Dock Vaults

The Princes Dock Vaults stood on the corner of Waterloo Road and Roberts Street. This 1908 photograph shows the pub displaying the manager Ernest Hall's name. The pub was not listed in the 1920s. The adjoining premises at 4 Waterloo Road was a PH named the Oxford that was listed to a ship's fender maker by 1912. The glass on the old gas light displays the street names.

International Hotel

The International Hotel stood at the junction of Waterloo Road and Galton Street. Prior to the 1880s, the premises was named the Waterloo Vaults. The licensee from 1903 to 1918 was William Eagles. The premises remained trading until closure in the 1950s. In the late 1970s, the building opened as the well known, dockside canteen, 'Frank's Cafe', that is still trading to date.

Police Report 1892: 'Back door opens into enclosed entry, the door of which when closed interferes with police supervision'.

Cork Hotel

This photograph from 1908, shows the Cork Hotel standing at the junction of Waterloo Road and the now abolished Barton Street. The manager's name, James H. Potter was displayed on the gable end of the premises. Before the 1870s, this pub was named the Dock Hotel, becoming the Trafalgar Vaults during the 1870s and 1890s, before taking its final name. By the 1920s, the premises was listed as dining rooms.

Waterloo Hotel

This pub is listed to Mrs Mary Doyle and, although known as Geraghtys Vaults, was named the Waterloo Hotel. when photographed in the 1890s. Standing at the junction of Waterloo, Road and Sligo Street, it was cleared, along with the rest of the block, before the First World War, for Bibby's mills. Other names of this pub were: 1840s Robert Burns and 1860s Bobby Burns. The adjoining Cottage PH, at 26 Waterloo Road can just be seen on the photograph. The premises was listed as Cocoa Rooms shortly before closure.

Anglo American Hotel

These premises, at the corner of Waterloo Road and Vandries Street, remain vacant to date, having had various uses since closing as a pub in approximately 1960. When the empty building next door was destroyed by fire in 1994, the former pub was left in isolation.

Trafalgar Hotel

At the junction of Waterloo Road and Vulcan Street, the Trafalgar Hotel was photographed during the 1920s when the manager was Tom McInerney. Before the 1880s, it was named the Langan Inn. Note the pre-letter telephone number 443, on the advertisement for Henderson and Glass. The premises closed as a PH in the 1930s and are presently in use as a cafe.

Trafalgar

This pub (below) was closed and displaying a for sale sign when photographed during the mid-1980s. However, a buyer was not required as the bulldozer moved in instead. Standing at the junction of Waterloo Road and Porter Street, it was named the Trafalgar since the 1930s, when the previous pub closed. Prior to this date, it was named the Waterford Arms and pre-1860s, the Scotch Highlander. The adjoining building, standing derelict to date, separates this pub from the previous one.

From Waterloo Road is the last named section of the Dock Road, Regent Road. This long road runs 1120 yards to the Bootle boundary, then 1601 yards through Bootle and originally contained over 30 public houses (approximately 30 in Liverpool, and 6 in Bootle).

Palatine Hotel

Standing on the corner of Regent Road and Dublin Street, this pub was a SV before the 1880s. Since this photograph was taken in the late 1980s, the then open premises have since been converted to a different business. Two magnificent dock side warehouses can be seen in this view. The nearest is the Stanley Dock Warehouse built in 1848 by Jesse Hartley, the renowned dock engineer. The other is the Stanley Dock Tobacco Warehouse, the largest of its type in the world when built in 1900. Both are presently in use as a huge Sunday market.

A1 At Lloyds

This view from 1908, shows the pub on the corner of Regent Road and Walter Street. Pre-1880s named the Clyde Vaults, the premises closed in the early 1990s and were demolished in 1995. 'A1 At Lloyds' referred to a ship considered by Lloyds, the insurance market, to be in first class condition. The implication was that the pub was equally first class.

Bramley Moore Hotel

Named after the facing dock (Sir John Bramley-Moore was a former Mayor (1848/49) and Chairman of the Dock Committee). In the 1840s, it was listed at 32 Regent Road as the Bramley Moore Dock Vaults. By the 1860s, it was listed as the North End House and from the 1870s, the Bramley Moore Hotel. In common with other Dock Road pubs, dwindling trade and the diminishing population of the area left it struggling to stay in business. Closed when photographed in the late 1980s, the premises have since reopened. The warehouse and chimneys of Clarence Dock power station have since been demolished.

American Hotel

Standing at the corner of Regent Road and Blackstone Street this pub had huge lettering on its facade when photographed in approximately 1903, when the licensee was Fras Aloyius Hennin. In common with many of its neighbouring pubs, the premises was closed and demolished during the 1980s.

Regent Hotel

Listed at 60 Regent Road, the photograph shows the pub closed and for sale in the mid-1980s. The premises was sold and reopened as Bonkers, the forerunner of a new trend of 'fun pubs'. The craze caught on throughout Merseyside, thriving for a while until the bubble burst causing the pub to close once again. It is currently closed. The pub was known locally as Mabels.

Police report 1892: 'Back door of public house and back door of shop adjoining open into enclosed entry, the door of which, if closed, would prevent the police having access to the back of the licensed premises'.

Convivial

Situated at the junction of Regent Street and Boundary Street, this photograph from the 1970s, shows the pub displaying a Whitbread's sign and the City's coat of arms, possibly indicating the fact that it was the first/last building of the old boundary of Liverpool and Kirkdale (see Boundary Street). The manageress at this time was Matilda Shillcock. During the mid-19th century, the premises had the unusual name of Ship Colonies and Commerce. In the 1870s, it was called the Dumbarton Castle and, from the 1890s, the Convivial. It is open to date and currently named Sherlocks. Before the 1970s, this pub was nicknamed Poison 'Arrys by dockers.

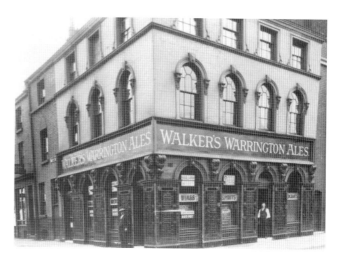

Edinburgh Castle

Listed at 91 Regent Road and 1 Boundary Street. This recent photograph, shows a cafe in a building which was previously a pub named the Edinburgh Castle which closed in the 1950s. Also featured on the block at 93 to 94 is the Sandon Lion which has recently reopened after closure.

Police reports 1892: 'Permitting drunkenness, dismissed (Edinburgh Castle). Permitting drunkenness, dismissed (Sandon Lion)'.

Atlantic

Sandhills Hotel

In the 1860s, these premises was listed as a WSV, then named the Sandhills Hotel from the 1890s to the 1930s. Its name changed to the Myrtle Hotel before returning to the Sandhills Hotel by 1940. The pub was rebuilt following war damage. The photograph from the 1920s shows the pub advertising Luncheons and Hot Pot in the window. The adjoining premises on Sandhills Lane was Davies' Cafe, which probably belonged to the pub's licensee, Robert Davies. The 1996 view, of the rebuilt premises, shows the pub derelict after a fire.

A rather rare view, nowadays, of three adjacent pubs that were all open when photographed in the 1980s. The Atlantic, displaying the defunct Higson's name at 162, is open to date. The Globe Boathouse (rebuilt), at the junction with Sandhills Lane, was formerly nicknamed Broken Nosed Jacks. This is open to date and has recently been renamed the Iron Horse. The Sandhills Hotel, at 160, is currently closed.

Dominion

This pub is open to date at 32 Bankfield Street. Before the 1880s, the premises was named the Dominion of North America and were listed at 32a Bankfield Street and 170 Regent Road. After 1880, the name shortened to the Dominion. A separate BH was originally listed under the premises, which became dining rooms in approximately 1912, and are still trading to date. A well known feature of this pub, is the statue of a 'settler and his dog looking out to sea, presumably towards America. When this photograph was taken, in approximately 1960, the manager was Stanley Brinton Phillips.

The following pubs although on Regent Road, were/are in Bootle, L20.

Victoria

This pub, at the corner of Regent Road and Howe Street, was listed as a BH in the 1860s. The photograph is from 1904, when the manager was Jacob Canon. The premises ceased trading as a pub in 1940 and began trading as a dock side cafe after the war. In 1998, the whole block became licensed once again and the premises is currently named the Regent Hotel. A date of 1864 can be seen on the facade of the block.

Carriers Dock Hotel

Also known as the Castle, this pub was located at the junction of Regent Road and a tiny street named Drake Street. The street still remains but only as an entrance to a factory and the site of the pub is now a small car park. Note the name Robsons over a former section of the pub, which was in use as dining rooms. The photograph, from 1912 when the licensee was Archie Sides, shows the adjoining former Harland and Wolff ship repairers which is currently derelict.

Millers Castle

Standing at the junction of Millers Bridge and Regent Road, this pub is currently named Ninas. This pre-First World War photograph shows the pub displaying the name Blezards on a window. The manager at this time was John Fletcher. On the far right of the photograph, the former Davenport's Dining Rooms (originally part of the pub) can be seen. The name of this pub and thoroughfare was taken from a residence with battlements built by a Liverpool solicitor, William Miller, in the 1820s. The mansion acquired the name Millers Castle. At that time, the pleasant north shore was a very different environment.

Langton Castle Hotel

The Langton Castle is a typical late 19th century building with
fine detail on its exterior. Listed at 76 Regent Road at its junction
with Nelson Street and currently closed. This view is from the
1950s when it was a Threlfall's house.

*The following two pubs were located in two of the former squalid
dockside streets that were once a common feature of the area.*

Mariners Arms

One of 12 pubs that traded in Regent Street, the Mariners Arms
(top right) stood at 49. Before 1860, it was named the Belfast
Arms and became a WSV in the 1880s before arriving at its final
name. A board above the window reads 'The Mariners Arms
Wine and Spirit Stores'. When photographed in the 1890s, the
licensee was Annie Tobin (probably the lady in the doorway).
Beyond a court entrance (no.6 court), the adjoining shop
advertises 'Quakers Brown Bread 2d and 3d'. The premises
closed in 1913 and only one pub, the Marco Polo, survived until
the 1950s.
Police Report 1903: 'Keeping open during prohibited hours.
Ordered to pay 4/6d and costs. Back door of licensed premises
and back door of adjoining premises open into enclosed entry, the
door of which, if closed, would interfere with police supervision.'

WSV

This photograph (opposite, bottom right) illustrates three common features of the old Dock Road area: warehouses, court property and an old WSV. Listed at 23 Denison Street, off Bath Street, this WSV was one of some 20 pubs that once existed in this street. Before the 1880s, it was named the Old Pilot Boat Tavern. The licensee was Elizabeth Beddows when this photograph was taken in the 1890s. The premises closed around 1914.

Adjoined the pub is a court (no.5). This was the street were Kitty Wilkinson lived (1786 to 1860). She worked incessantly for the poor, taking in their cholera-ridden clothes and washing them in her own humble home. Through her tireless work, she became one of the instigators behind the opening of the world's first public wash-house at Upper Frederick Street. This wash-house, along with others that sprung up over the city, was a godsend for the inhabitants of court property, where water was a rare commodity. The squalid Denison Street and surrounding area is long gone and the site is now a modern industrial site. One remnant of old Denison Street is a public house, the King Edward (see Great Howard Street).

Since the construction of the north docks, no licensed pubs existed on the north dock estate, although for many years there was a floating nightclub named the Clubship Landfall. Many readers will recall this 'club', which was originally a landing craft tank, number LCT 7074. It was one of hundreds that took part in the D-Day invasion during the Second World War. The actual part played during the war by such craft has largely been ignored by military historians and sadly, after closure as a nightclub, this rare specimen was laid up for years in a derelict condition in Collingwood Dock. Although used as a night club (Clubship Landfall) from 1968, the vessel had in fact been registered as a club shortly after the Second World War under the name Landfall, an exclusive clubhouse of the Merseyside Master Mariners Club berthed in Canning Dock. After thriving throughout the 1950s, a gradual decline set in throughout the 1960s, when economic changes and dwindling membership, caused this exclusive club to fold. With the closure of the south docks in 1972, the vessel was moved north to Collingwood Dock. In the late 1970s, with its location out of the city centre and the decline of the immediate vicinity, closure was inevitable. This 1994 view shows the vessel located in Collingwood Dock, its number covered by rust. Even the dock wall is crumbling. At the time of writing, the vessel has been removed to Birkenhead Docks, hopefully to be restored for future generations.

The huge number of pubs that lined the Dock Road were frequented mainly by dockers, seamen and dock-related workers. Considering there were nearly 20,000 dockers alone, it is not surprising that so many pubs existed.

The next main road from the Dock Road is Great Howard Street; named after the social reformer, John Howard, who was involved in the building of the borough gaol in 1786. It remains a major thoroughfare for traffic travelling to and from the city centre, although its former status as a busy industrial area is diminished. The pubs that still remain are considerably less in number from the sixty or more that once stood here before the Second World War.

During the last century, Great Howard Street led directly into Old Hall Street (King Edward Street was not yet in existence) and the whole vicinity was a most squalid area. The construction of the new King Edward Street swept away many of the old slums and created a widened and improved Leeds Street, Old Hall Street and Great Howard Street. The atrocious slums of the area, however, did not vanish overnight and it took many years before they were all cleared. Over the last ten years, both Leeds Street and King Edward Street have once again changed. Both are now wide main thoroughfares, where landscaping replaces the pubs, house and shops that once lined them. The former, huge Bibby's Plant on Great Howard Street, has been demolished and the site is presently a mixture of landscaping and modern buildings. (Although currently still so-named, Great Howard Street and its continuation, Derby Road, have recently been incorporated into Atlantic Avenue).

This is a general cargo 'McClan' boat, berthed in the Alexandra Dock. Although general cargo ships still trade, they are greatly reduced in numbers.The cargo of locomotives and their tenders (waiting to be loaded for export to Burma) are themselves, of course, now just a memory.

The following were/are on Great Howard Street.
West side 1 to 189 were/are in Liverpool 3, the remainder in Liverpool 5.

Trafalgar Wine and Spirit Vaults

This long closed pub was listed at 17 Great Howard Street at its junction with Gibraltar Row. It has had a number of previous names: Rose and Thistle 1840s, Manchester and Bolton Tavern 1860s, Ship Inn 1870s. Not listed 1908. This photograph was taken shortly before closure, when the licensee was Thomas Hayhurst. Note the policeman apparently unaware of the photographer.

Athletic Vaults

This old dilapidated property stood on the corner of Great Howard Street and Denison Street. It was previously named the

Clarrington Vaults in the 1890s, the Shamrock in the 1880s and The Balarat and Melbourne Vaults in the 1860s. The building was demolished in the early years of this century when King Edward Street was laid out and a new pub, the King Edward was built on the same site. This pub is open to date. This view is from approximately 1908, when the manager's name, P. Quinn (Patrick), was displayed over a window. A tallow chandlers is located next door where three children look inquisitively at the photographer. Above the shop, there are faded advertisements for 'Coleman's Mustard' and 'H.P. Sauce'. The shop adjoining, on Great Howard Street, was listed to George Walton, bread and flour dealer.

King Edward

The previous pub's replacement, the King Edward, can be seen on this photograph from the 1970s. It is now set back off the aforementioned line of Great Howard Street. The former Northern Hospital, on the corner of Leeds Street, is shown on the right. Part of the site of the hospital now houses a recently opened car showroom.

Alexandra Vaults

Before the 1860s, this pub (top right), standing at the corner of Great Howard Street and Galton Street, was called the Branch Vaults. It was then named the Grapes until the 1890s, after which it was called the Alexandra Vaults until its closure in the 1950s, as part of an extension of Bibbys. The 1920's photograph features the long demolished former dwellings of Galton Street and the manager John Watson. The site is currently landscaped.

Goat Hotel

These premises, which are open to date and located at the junction of Great Howard Street and Regent Street, have been so named since approximately 1914. Before this, the pub had a number of names: 1840s Sir Walter Scott; 1850s Lamb and Flag; 1860s to 1880s the Glass Barrel; then, somewhat strangely, for a few years around 1890 resuming to Sir Walter Scott; It can be safely presumed that rebuilding will have occurred at least once. The premises are known locally as Gormleys after a former manager, William A Gormley, who was licensee from the 1930s to approximately 1950.

Police Report 1892: 'Selling drink to a drunken man to pay 4/6 costs. Back door of public house and back door of adjoining premises open into enclosed entry, the door of which closed would prevent the access of the police into the rear of the licensed premises'.

Coach and Horses

Listed at the corner of Great Howard Street and Carlton Street, the building, which closed in approximately 1960, was last in use as a betting shop but is currently empty. Carlton Street was one of the worst of Liverpool's Victorian slums and contained atrocious court property which persisted well into this century. (The 1960s saw the last of the courts). When this photograph was taken in the 1920s, the licensee was Henry Ellis. Before closure the premises was known locally as Wynnes.

Brown Cow

The photograph (below left) is from 1912, when the manager was Sydney O'Brien, features a once common sight of dockside streets, a sign giving directions to the various docks. This one reads 'Dublin Street leading to Clarence Dock and Clarence Graving Dock' (removed on the modern view). Before the 1880s, this pub, listed at the corner of Great Howard Street and Dublin Street, was named the Black Cow (probably in connection with livestock brought from the docks). Locally known as Jack Wills, it is currently closed. The 1990s view (below) features the magnificent Bonded Tea Warehouses on Great Howard Street (1880s) and warehouses in Dublin Street, that still remain.

Bull Inn

The Bull Inn, which is open to date, is listed at 181a Great Howard Street and 2 Dublin Street. When it was photographed in approximately 1914, the licensee was Edward Tobin. The houses on Dublin Street were cleared by the 1960s to make way for modern warehouses. The adjoining block to the pub on Great Howard Street was also demolished, leaving the premises currently in isolation.

The following were/are on the east side: 2 to 180 were/are in Liverpool 3, the remainder in Liverpool 5.

O'Gormans Bar

This pub formerly stood on the corner of Great Howard Street and Sprainger Street. Before the 1870s, it was listed as a SV. In the 1870s, it was named Dodds Vaults after the manager, Thomas Dodd. In the late 1980s, its name changed to O'Gormans Bar. In 1994, the pub was closed and demolished, along with the large silo and warehouses as part of the huge redevelopment of the area. Prior to closure, the pub was known locally as McCabes.

Trafalgar Arms

This photograph of the Trafalgar Arms (opposite top), listed at the junction of Great Howard Street and Upper William Street, was taken in 1905, when the manager was Henry Chambers. Before the 1880s, the pub was named the Freemasons Arms. When the premises ceased trading as a pub, in approximately 1960, it was known locally as Mary Williams (a former licensee). It later became a post office and was demolished in 1997. Police Report 1903: 'Selling drink to a drunken man 20/- plus costs'.

British Queen Vaults

This pub (opposite bottom) was formerly a WSV, listed at the junction of Maddrell Street (originally Slate Street). This photograph, from 1908 when the manager was James Hamilton, shows its facade on the Great Howard Street side and the words 'Bradys TE Branch'. The adjoining shop belonged to David Rule, provision merchants. By 1931, the former pub was listed to Mrs Mary May, fried fish dealer. Police Report 1892: 'Allowing gaming. 4/6d plus costs.

Royal Oak

Photographed in the 1920s, the Royal Oak stood at 256 -258 Great Howard Street at its junction with Lightbody Street. A court entrance can be seen adjoining the pub in Lightbody Street. The site is now landscaped. The adjoining shop, 260 - 262, were Cocoa Rooms, listed to Mrs Helen Kingan. Not listed 1940s.

Louth Arms

Listed at the corner of Great Howard Street and Athol Street, the Louth Arms closed in the early 1970s and the premises have only recently been demolished. Before the 1890s, the pub had the unusual name of Souter Johnnys Vaults. Managed by Thomas Gorman when photographed in 1908, the adjoining shop was listed to Mrs Nellie Hughes, greengrocer. Before closure, the premises was known locally as Peter Sages.

Police Report 1903: 'Selling drink to a drunken man. Dismissed . Selling drink to a drunken man. 20 Shillings plus costs.'

Neptune Vaults

Listed at 298 Great Howard Street and 1 Athol Street. Photographed in 1912, when the manager was James William Arthur, the adjoining barbers can be seen advertising a '4d hair cut'. The windows of the pub display the names 'Harding and Parrington' and 'John Joule and Sons Stone Ale'. These were Brewers from Stone, Staffordshire, who were taken over by Harding and Parrington in 1873. Not listed 1930s.

Albion Hotel

This site, at the corner of Great Howard Street and Blackstone Street, is now a Chinese restaurant and wholesalers. This photograph from 1912, when the manager was John Timoney, shows a court entrance in Blackstone Street. The shop in Great Howard Street was listed to Thomas Coulon, confectioner. The premises was locally known as Dustins and, in the 1950s, listed as the Albion Social Club. Listed 1970.

Woodman Inn

Victoria

Before the 1890s these premises, listed at 374-376 Great Howard Street and 1 Townsend Street, were a WSV. When photographed in 1908, the manager was Robert S. Crellin. Listed 1964.

Listed at 342 Great Howard Street and 11 Blackstone Street, this view is from approximately 1965, when the licensee was Richard James Murray. Described in 1892 as having three entrances: one in Great Howard Street, one in Blackstone Street and one in number 1 court, Blackstone Street. Listed 1970. The site is now landscaped.

The final demise of industry is within living memory. Long established factories (notably Tate and Lyle, British American Tobacco Co, and Tillotsons) closed, ending a tradition where generations of families had worked together. This view from the 1970s, shows a portion of Tate and Lyle from Chadwick Street to Love Lane. The site is now a mixture of landscaping and modern housing.

The Great Howard Street/Vauxhall Road vicinity was a major industrial area surrounded by atrocious housing. This is a typical scene from 1913, showing a railway goods yard and numerous chimneys belonging to the many industries that once traded in the area. The coal yards, gas works, foundries, glass and pottery manufacturers, tan yards, vitriol works, soaperies, alkali works, lime works and numerous other mills and breweries are now long forgotten.

During the build-up of industry in the 19th century, businesses sometimes helped to clear some of the early slums, particularly because land was needed for the railway as was the case in the photograph above. A number of slum ridden streets existed on this site pre-1870s.

At the junction of Waterloo Road and Stewart Street was a pub named George IV. Stewart Street was a most squalid dock side street containing some 44 courts. Six other pubs existed amongst the squalor of this long forgotten street. All were cleared when the London and North Western Railway goods station was extended in the 1870s.

Vauxhall Road

The third main road eastward, after the Dock Road and Great Howard Street, is Vauxhall Road (originally Pinfold Lane) whose side streets were once a teeming slum area. In common with all the older parts of the town, the road contained public houses galore that serviced the once densely populated area.

It is hard to imagine nowadays, particularly with the recently built Eldonian Estate and present improvements that, until the early years of the twentieth century, more than 70 PHs were listed on this road making it second only to Scotland Road for the number of pubs it once contained. The road probably contained more pubs during the last century than traced because, amongst the many industrial premises, there stood numerous breweries where a number of unlicensed long forgotten dives would have existed in conjunction with some of the smaller brewers. For example, the following were listed without numbers in the 1840s: Thomas Humphreys (beer, hay and straw dealer); Robert Ainscough (SV and coal dealer); Joseph Barton (WSV and soda water manufacturer); William Rockliff (B.H and millwright) Throughout the century, the names James and Joseph Ackers (brewers) were frequently found at various addresses connected with breweries or BHs along the road. Also, in common with the town in general during the 19th century, were local shop-fronted drinking dens,their names now lost in history.

The west side of the road alone once contained over 30 pubs with only one remaining, the Vauxhall Vaults, known locally as Dangsters. The majority of the pubs had closed by the First World War and, by the 1960s only 13 remained.

The following were on the west side: 1 to 227 were/are in Liverpool 3, the remainder in Liverpool 5.

Bulls Head

This view from 1893 shows the pub on the right, standing at the corner of Vauxhall Road and Burlington Street.This is a typical Liverpool scene of that era; barefooted children who would have certainly just come out of the Bulls Head with jugs of ale for their parents. In 1912, the premises was listed as Cocoa Rooms with the adjoining shop listed to a tobacconist.

Over measure beer may appeal to the customer but in Victorian times, it encouraged children as young as eight or nine years old to drink beer, as the following report from a meeting of Brewers, Spirit Merchants and Licensed Victuallers held at the Concert Hall, Lord Nelson Street in 1869 states: 'The over measure system encourages servant girls to become drunkards and children as well, because when they got over measure, they could drink some of the liquor without being discovered. He has known in his own experience, children from eight to nine years of age drinking the beer before they took it home to their parents, who were even then satisfied with the measure they had received'.

Another speaker insisted that 'This pernicious system of over-measure has a great deal to do with bringing people into trouble' and the third (Mr James Mellor, brewer) declared that 'the over measure practise was a means of converting every cottage into a school for drunkenness, because it taught the rising generation the taste of beer at a very early age'. The law eventually banned children from pubs in 1904.

Opposite top Aerial view of British American Tobacco factory on Commercial Road c1950
Opposite bottom Tate and Lyle sugar refining factory on Vauxhall Road.

Rutland Hotel

Listed at 185 Vauxhall Road and 2 Charters Street (abolished), these premises was named the Branch Vaults from the 1840s to the 1860s. They were then listed as a 'ginger beer dealer' until the 1890s. A section of a garden centre, built in conjunction with modern housing, now stands on this site. The pub's name is clearly displayed along with the manager's, Patrick Redmond, when photographed in the 1890s. The area has undergone a complete environmental change from when this pub was thriving. Not listed 1908. It later became a social club named Bottomleys. The adjoining shop was listed to John Oldham, tripe dresser.

14 courts and 6 pubs once existed on the right hand side of Charters Street between Vauxhall Road and the bridge, with the opposite side consisting of coal yards that lined a former cut of the Liverpool – Leeds Canal.

The following were/are on the east side. Numbers 2 to 204a were/ are in Liverpool 3, the remainder in Liverpool 5:

Naylor Hotel

Before the 1890s, this pub, standing at the junction of Vauxhall Road and Naylor Street, was named the Liverpool Arms. In this 1920's photograph, old housing and warehouses of Naylor Street can be seen. The manager at this time was James Kirwan. The premises closed in the 1950s and the building is currently in use as a different business.

Lamb and Flag

Listed at 92 Vauxhall Road and currently a general store, the premises was formerly a public house named the Lamb and Flag, which closed in approximately 1904. Amongst various uses since, it has been the Liverpool Working Men's Conservative Association: 1920s. Police Report 1903 'Quoits and domino playing allowed'.

WSV

This old establishment, formerly listed at the junction of Vauxhall Road and Paul Street, lost its licence in 1905. It was managed by John Roberts when photographed in the 1890s. A bare-footed boy can be seen outside the adjoining British Workman Public House Co. Ltd. (Once part of the pub and listed as dining rooms in the 1930s). Although the building still remains, extensive alterations have left it unrecognisable as the former pub.

The Feathers

Open to date at 106 to 108 Vauxhall Road at its junction with Paul Street. Earlier named The Liver, this photograph was taken in 1912.

Green Flag

Listed at Vauxhall Road's junction with Blackstock Street, the premises was closed in the 1920s to make way for a municipal housing scheme, Blackstock Gardens. They have since been replaced by modern industrial units. The actual site of the pub when replaced was listed to the Transport and General Workers Union (building shown on the photograph right top).

Eagle

Open to date at 1-3 Blackstock Street at its junction with Vauxhall Road. This view shows the pub before the First World War, when it was named the Eagle Vaults. Old houses on Blackstock Street can be seen along with an adjoining barber's shop which displays 'This is Ridewoods Hairdressing Rooms'. The manager at the time was Martin Carney. During the 1890s, the premises was listed as the Eagle Vaults and United Distilleries Co. Ltd.

The second photograph shows the pub during the early 1960s when the manager was Cornelius Biggenden. The houses of Blackstock Street have been cleared and replaced by industrial

units whilst the adjoining barbers shop stands empty. Note the lorry, belonging to the British Road Services, parked in Blackstock Street. The pub is currently named the Eagle Cons.

Fail-Me-Never

This unusually named pub, listed at the junction of Vauxhall Road and Arley Street, was named the Mountain Dew before the 1860s. When photographed in 1910, the manager was David Telford. The premises closed in the early 1960s and were then listed as a betting shop prior to demolition.

Arley Inn

On the corner of Vauxhall Road and Arley Street, the pub was previously listed as a SD in the 1860s and a WSV up to the 1890s. The 1920's photograph shows two well dressed children on the right, probably the licensee's, Michael Carroll's daughters, whilst the children on the left are bare-footed. The premises was demolished in 1971 for the new Kingsway Tunnel. The view of Arley Street dwellings just before the First World War, shows property that would be classed as unfit nowadays, although it had, in fact, been built to replace horrendous slums in 1897. They were known as 'Scotch Houses'. Terraced property is still abundant throughout Liverpool, although this type no longer exists. Two front doors for two dwellings are common, these houses feature groups of four front doors. The centre doors led directly upstairs to separate rooms above. These dwellings were cleared in the 1960s.

Glass House

The Glass House is open to date and listed at 198 Vauxhall Road and Bond Street, taking the block up between Bond Street and Eldon Street. So named since the 1860s, this pub took its name from a large glass works that was situated in Bond Street. As can be seen in this 1920's photograph, it was one of the few pubs of the period to advertise lager. The manager at the time was John Brereton.

Police Report 1898: 'New sanitary conveniences have been provided since the last annual licensing meeting. Plans were not submitted to the justices'.

Black Dog

These premises, at the corner of Vauxhall Road and Burlington Street, were listed as a brewery (183 Burlington Street) in the 1840s. By the 1860s, there was a brewery and PH named the Victoria at the current address. The brewery closed in the 1870s and the premises was then listed as the British Workman Provision Co. The premises was not listed in 1908, the date of the photograph, when the pub had been renamed the Black Dog and was managed by Richard J. Wall. The name Black Dog was retained until closure in approximately 1970. The premises are currently trading as a betting shop and the adjoining church hall in Burlington Street, a former Welsh chapel, also remains.

Green Man and Queens Arms

The Green Man is still trading on the corner of Vauxhall Road and Green Street (originally Kent Street North). Like Portland Street, Green Street was once court-ridden but now contains modern houses. Before the 1870s, this pub was listed as a BH and, during the 1870s, was named the Green Man Still. By the 1890s, its name was changed to the Green Man Inn. This view from the 1960s, also shows the rebuilt Queens Arms, standing at the junction of Vauxhall Road and Portland Street. Before the 1880s, this pub was named the Portland House. The premises is currently closed.

Police Report 1892: 'Back door of licensed premises and back door of one private house open into an enclosed entry, the door of which when closed would prevent the police having free access to the back of the licensed premises'(Queens Arms). 1902: 'selling drink to a drunken man. 20/ and costs'(Green Man).

Castle

The Castle, on the corner of Vauxhall Road and Tatlock Street, has been so-named since the 1860s and is open to date. This view from 1995 shows the demolition of neighbouring high rise flats. Houses have since been constructed on the site.

Jamaica

Still trading at the junction of Vauxhall Road and Hopwood Street (which has recently been renamed Gem Street at the Vauxhall Road end, after a former local cinema, the Gem, that stood in nearby Vescock Street). Before the 1880s, the premises was a BH. The pub itself has long been known locally as the Rat. This view, from 1911, was taken during the General Transport Strike and the X by the group of men in the middle of Vauxhall Road marks the spot were a man had been shot dead by troops. By the 1920s, Walker had replaced Blezard as the brewers. The licensee in 1911 was William Gertey with James Francis Melia licensee from the 1920s until the 1950's.

Neptune Hotel

The Neptune was listed at 340-342 Vauxhall Road at its junction with Burnett Street, (originally Ivy Street) and closed in the 1950s. The 1980's view shows the premises standing derelict after they ceased trading as a betting shop. The premises have since been demolished.

Coach and Horses

Before the 1880s, this pub, listed at 362-364 Vauxhall Road at its junction with Slade Street (now abolished) was named the Jamaica Vaults. This photograph is from the 1920s, when the manager was James Newall. The pub closed in the early 1960s and the premises was listed to a shopkeeper in 1964 prior to demolition.

Despite the tremendous number of pubs that once lined Vauxhall Road, few were on the west side between Burlington Street and Boundary Street because of the number of as industrial premises. This view features the only listed building that existed on the road. The large turret-like structure that looks like the remains of a castle, was part of the former Fairrie sugar refinery, built in 1847. Listed status did not save this building which was photographed in the 1980s during demolition.

They say everything turns full circle and this tranquil scene from 1814, of the bridge over Chisenhale Street from Vauxhall Road.

is a prime example of this. There are no other buildings on the street and it can be presumed that fish would have been plentiful in the clear flowing waters of the canal. Within a couple of decades, the tranquil scene was transformed completely. Gone was the windmill and, between Vauxhall Road and the canal, some 26 courts and six public houses were in existence. Demolition took place as early as the 1890s when some of the courts and 4 of the pubs (numbers 16, 18, 24, and 33) were cleared. A police station was also built in the street at that time. By the 1990s, once again, only one structure exists. Gone are the courts, police station and pubs and, after some 150 years of industrial waste and sewerage pouring into the filthy canal, it is being cleaned and replenished with fish once again. Since the 1990s, the right hand side of the street has been built-up with houses and bungalows. Many are named 'courts', but I doubt if many of the younger residents will have even heard of the original, atrocious court property once abundant in this vicinity.

CHISENHALE STREET BRIDGE AND MILL.
1814

Eldon Vaults

Listed at the corner of Eldon Street and Limekiln Lane and photographed in 1910, with the manager's name clearly displayed and a typical street urchin of the time standing bare-footed in the doorway.

Police Report 1903: 'Permitting drunkenness. Dismissed'.

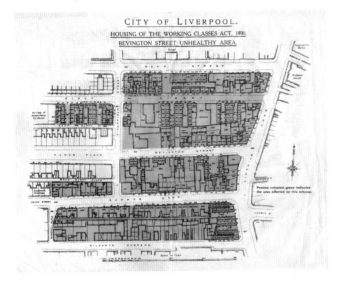

Two maps of the vicinity featuring the huge slum clearance undertaken by the council in the early 20th century. This was one of the largest schemes of the time in Liverpool and in a council report of 1913 featuring the progress in housing, the following extract was recorded: 'If they provide the people with plenty of private houses it is the best antidote for the existence of public-houses. In Liverpool thirty years ago, there used to be a school of reformers whose idea of progress was, roughly, this: public-housing the men, warehousing the women and children and workhousing the aged'.

Fleece

A former WSV, listed at 84 Eldon Street at its junction with Titchfield Street, these premises was named the Lamb before the 1880s. Not listed 1912. Photographed in approximately 1908, when the manager was Patrick Conway.

The 1912 photograph below shows typical slum property shown on the map. This was part of Eldon Street, featuring courts 5, 7 and 9.

This 1912 view shows the completion of the new tenements. Located in Eldon Grove (not yet named on the map but listed as a new roadway), note the playgrounds, one for boys and one for girls. The band stand in the centre was constantly in use for the residents. Performances were given twice a week during the summer months. One notable modern scourge is missing - vandalism. The same blocks in 1997 can be seen in the photograph (top right) empty and boarded up. The band stand and shelters have long gone and the playground is just a waste ground. Although built to replace slums, this type of property is now obsolete. They were recently used as students flats although, being currently empty, their future is uncertain.

The photograph below shows a kitchen-cum-bedroom of a house in the Bevington Street insanitary area, although not specific, it is typical of such property. I wonder how many slept in the bed?

The old slums of Summer Seat were cleared and replaced with quite a modern looking block of self contained cottages for their time. Testimony to them is they still remain to date.

Rising Sun

Open to date (having been re-built), the Rising Sun, one of originally ten pubs in the street, was listed at 124 Portland Street. This 1986 view shows Portland Gardens, municipal housing that has since been demolished. New housing occupies the site and the pub is now addressed at Green Street, which used to run parallel to Portland Street when the old property existed.

It may seem strange nowadays that members of the clergy would have owned licensed premises in the 1890s, yet quite a few did. The registered owner of this pub in 1892 was the Rev Thomas Lowe, whose address was Rockleigh House, Tranmere.

Other examples of public house ownership in 1892 include the
following examples:

York Hotel, 6 Boundary Street
Licensee: Joseph Smart. Registered owner Andrew Brown,
brassfounder.
Griffin, 52 Derby Road and 2 Bankfield Street.
Licensee: Annie McCubbin. Registered owner David McCubbin,
30 Lower Bank View.
Union, 81 Commercial Road and 42 Sandhills Lane.
Licensee: Issac Dickenson. Registered owner Robert Blezard,
brewer, Scotland Road.
Stanley Bar, 99 Stanley Road.
Licensee: Charles Curley. Registered owner Daniel Higson and
Co. brewers, Cheapside.
Knowsley, 329 Stanley Road.
Licensee: Samuel H Gardham. Registered owner Robert Blezard,
brewer, Scotland Road.
Hamlet, 1 Kirkdale Road and 249 Boundary Street
Licensee: John Sullivan. Registered owner Exors. of Thomas
Estell Albert Ragg, Abbortsford Road, Great Crosby.
Alexandra, 129 Kirkdale Road.
Licensee: Benjamin Hay. Registered owner D Smart and Co.

brewers, Chaucer Street.
Phoenix, 48 Foley Street.
Licensee: Charles Organ. Registered owner Mary A Heyes, St
Mary's View, Huyton.

Amongst the many pubs that once thrived along Vauxhall Road
are the following, most of which disappeared in the early years of
the twentieth century:

22-24 Cart and Horses
40 Plume of Feathers
49-51 Genus Britain
101 Tim Bobbin
119 Eaton Hall
158 Emerald Isle
162 Blind Beggar
183a Castle of Comfort
274a Tam O'Shanter
276 North Pole Vault

Walton Road once boasted three cinemas. The Victory located at the junction of Luton Grove, opened in 1922 and was apparently named from the 'victory' after the Great War. 'The Glenn Miller Story' was showing when this photograph was taken in the 1950s. The Victory closed in 1961 and the site was replaced by a row of shops. The other two cinemas were the Astoria, which closed in 1974 and currently in use as a bingo hall, and the Queens, which closed in 1959 and has since been demolished.

Kirkdale/Walton

Kirkdale is an ancient settlement recorded in the Domesday book as 'Churchedale'. However, in common with many former townships around Liverpool, growth was slow until the 19th century. The population of Kirkdale in 1831, was only 2562 rising to 57668 by 1881. The district of Kirkdale is difficult to define with postal districts because it includes L4, L5, and L20, (L20 is also a district of Bootle). The Scotland Road area, although classed as Kirkdale, is rarely referred to as such whilst L4 also covers part of Walton and Anfield, with L5 also covering Everton. Therefore, for the purpose of this publication we start at Boundary Street (the ancient boundary of Liverpool and Kirkdale) northward.

The following were/are in Boundary Street, which originally contained 21 pubs:

York Hotel

This pub was listed at 6 Boundary Street at its junction with Fulton Street, close to the Dock Road. Before the 1880s, it was named the Wellington Vaults. The writing on the window in this 1908 photograph, is 'Importers and Bonders of Wines and Spirits'. The manager at this time was John Richards. During the 1920s, the premises was sold by Walker to Threlfall and ceased trading as a PH just after the Second World War. Last in use as a betting shop, it is currently standing empty as can be seen in the view from the 1990s. The building on the right of this photograph is Sherlocks PH (shown more clearly in the Dock Road section). Police Report 1903: 'Supplying liquor to a police constable when on duty. £5 and costs'.

Great Britain

As indicated by the architecture of the building, this was one of the older Boundary Street pubs and was formerly listed at the street's junction with Darwen Street (now abolished). Before the First World War the licensee was Edward Weatherby. The pub closed in the 1920s.

Cheshire Lines

This pub stood at the junction of Bundary Street and the now abolished New Hedley Street. The cellar of the adjoining house was in business as a shop when this photograph was taken in the 1920s. It was named after the nearby railway (it was also named the Midland and Cheshire Lines Hotel from the 1870s until the 1890s). Before the 1870s, it was named the Thomaston Hotel. Listed 1964.

Alexandra

This huge pub was listed at Boundary Street's junction with Heriot Street. Listed 1964. Landscaping that fronts modern houses now occupies this site.

Police Report 1899: 'Selling drink to a drunken man (October) Dismissed. Selling drink to a drunken man (November) 40/- and costs. Conviction quashed by Recorder'.

This photograph, taken in 1991, shows housing and a multi-storey block off Boundary Street, that were only some 20 years old, in the process of demolition. The street was Barmouth Street on which corner one of the street's pubs, the Clock, once stood. Along with the original housing of the vicinity, the pub is just a memory. During the demolition, a modern pub, the Leprechaun, was also cleared.

The street was part of the area known locally as 'over the bridge', referring to the Leeds – Liverpool Canal bridge. At the time of writing, the area has once again been built up with new housing, which, hopefully, will not be pulled down after only 20 years.

Heriot Arms

Listed at 51 Heriot Street, off Boundary Street, junction of Latham Street. The 1920's photograph shows customers peering out of the door and a small crowd of inquisitive people looking towards the cameraman. The pub survived the mass demolition programme of the 1960s and 1970s although, since the early 1990s, the pub has opened and closed on a number of occasions. It is currently closed.

The continuation of Great Howard Street, just beyond Boundary Street, is Derby Road through into Bootle, (at one time containing 31 pubs, 12 in Liverpool, 19 in Bootle). The following were/are located here:

Cottage

Listed at 2 Derby Road, this pub was named the Victoria Cottage (Derby Road was then named Victoria Road) before the 1890s. The Cottage was a well frequented local surrounded by housing and industry. The premises, photographed in 1972, were demolished in 1994. Landscaping now covers the site.

Wellington

The Wellington was at the junction of Derby Road and Bankfield Street. This photograph is from 1905, when the manager was Adam Wallace. The pub was demolished during the 1960s and part of the site became Silcock's animal feed offices. This ugly modern building stood derelict for 15 years until 1996 and was so much of an eye-sore that before demolition a large poster was placed on the premises stating: 'Now you see it, soon you won't'.

Griffin Hotel

The Griffin Hotel stands at the corner of Derby Road and Bankhall Street. Photographed in 1908, when the manager was William Wilson. Opening and closing at various times, the premises currently stand closed. The adjoining warehouse in Bankhall Street remains, having a date of 1863 on its facade.

Royal Alhambra

These large premises, standing at the junction of Derby Road and Esk Street, ceased trading as a pub in the 1970s. The building was open as another business when photographed in 1995 but has since been demolished. The wall next to the parked lorry on Derby Road is all that remains of a former Bridewell although, with the current large scale redevelopment in progress, this too will probably be demolished. Such an unusual name (the only one in Liverpool) derives from a palace in the Granada province of Spain, built some 700 years ago. In the 15th century, southern Spain was under Moslem rule. At that time, a long drawn out advance of Christian power in Europe gradually rolled back the Moorish stronghold. This culminated in the end of over seven centuries of rule by the Moslems in 1492, with the fall of Granada, their last stronghold. The Palace itself had been built by both the Moors and Spanish.

Knowsley Arms

This pub was situated on the corner of Derby Road and William Henry Street. When photographed in approximately 1912, the licensee was George Robbins and the pub was known locally as the Blue House. The building in William Henry Street was a shoeing and forge-yard listed to G. Rawsthorn. The premises was closed and demolished in the early 1990s as part of the scheme to widen Derby Road.

Marine

Standing at the junction of Derby Road and Raleigh Street, the premises ceased trading as a pub in the 1980s and, as shown, was last in use as a cafe, aptly named the Marine. This view from 1996, features the whole block standing derelict and awaiting demolition as part of the huge regeneration of the road. At the other end of the block, at the junction of Beresford Street (now demolished), was a pub named the Prince of Wales.

The two streets, along with Dundas Street, led between Derby Road and Regent Road, close to the boundary with Liverpool, which was probably the most notorious part of the borough in the late 19th century. These three streets, in particular, may have contributed to the old description of 'brutal Bootle'. A reference from the Health Committee in 1882 was: 'to the reckless class of inhabitants of Lyons Street, Dundas Street and Raleigh Street'. Lyons Street was described in the Bootle Times as 'the worst thoroughfare in the borough and, on many occasions, its name has figured in the local annals of crime'.

The old slum houses of the streets are now long gone. Raleigh Street now contains industrial premises. Dundas Street has disappeared whilst Lyons Street has changed names to Beresford Street and is now just a few yards in length.

Bootle Irish National Club

Established in 1899, the Irish Club was originally located on the other side of Derby Road at its junction with Pleasant Street. In 1909, it ceased trading and became dining rooms. In 1911, the club moved across the road to the junction of Raleigh Street, taking over a former pawnbrokers at 280. It remained at this address until 1960, when it moved to its current site between Effingham Street and Howe Street, reopening in 1962.

Returning to Kirkdale, the continuation of Vauxhall Road at Boundary Street is Commercial Road where the following were/are, from a total of nine pubs: The following two were on the west side:

Boundary Vaults

These premises, listed as a BH before the 1890s, stood on the corner of Commercial Road and Boundary Street. Adjoining, at 3 Boundary Street, was the Spread Eagle, with a seperate SV at 5. By the 1890s, numbers 1 and 3 had amalgamated as the Boundary Vaults. When photographed in approximately 1908, the manager was Thomas Davies. The premises bore a sign that read 'Boundary Street thoroughfare to Bramley Moore, Wellington and Sandon Docks'. Not listed in the 1940s.

Union Hotel

Situated on the corner of Commercial Road and Sandhills Lane. When photographed during the 1920s, the premises was owned by Barker's Huyton Ales. The pub was known locally as Lowes, after a former manager (Frederick). The adjoining sweet shop to the right of the pub has long been demolished. The site of the sweet shop later became a scrap yard which was cleared in the early 1990s. Closure of the pub became inevitable when it was left in isolation and demolition followed in 1997.

The British American Tobacco Company was one of the last standing large factories of the area, once employing thousands of people. It occupied most of the west side of Commercial Road between Boundary Street and Sandhills Lane.

The factory started business in 1908 on the site of an earlier foundry and disused coal merchants, with the first wing operational in 1912. The factory closed and left the city in 1991. Before closure, the company had invested a large amount of money in the building and since leaving, a number of plans for usage have been suggested, including dividing the premises into smaller units. However, as this view from 1997 shows, the structure is in the process of demolition, although a section is apparently to be saved.

Great Mersey

Standing at the junction of Commercial Road and Great Mersey Street, the pub is currently the only building on the road on its eastern side. Photographed in the late 1980s when still open, the premises is currently a different business.

Police Report 1892: 'Selling drink to a drunken woman. 20/- and costs'.

Evelyn Hotel

Photographed in the 1960s, the Evelyn Hotel, an Ind Coope house, stood at 78 Commercial Road at its junction with Evelyn Street. Prior to demolition in the 1970s, it was known locally as Kellys. The modern housing shown on this view has also been demolished. The site of this and the next two pubs is now the edge of a football pitch.

Police Report 1903: 'Permitting drunkenness. Dismissed'.

Sandhills Hotel

Sandhills Bridge Inn

Photographed in the 1960s, when the manager was William McArthur, this pub was listed at 134 Commercial Road at its junction with Aspinall Street. The small shop adjoining the pub in Aspinall Street was named Dunns and a friend of mine, Dominic Whelan, who lived in this neighbourhood recalls how, during the 1950s and 60s, it was referred to as 'a little gold mine', opening late every night and one of the few shops during that era to open on a Sunday. Listed 1970.

Reading

This former Higson's house stood on the corner of Commercial Road and Rockingham Street. When photographed during the early 1960s, the manager was Michael Thomas Whearty. The premises was known locally as Speeds. Listed 1970.

This old view is from the 1890s, when the licensee was William Moore. Standing on the corner of Commercial Road and Reading Street, the pub survived the mass demolition of the vicinity during the 1970s, only to succumb to the bulldozer in the 1980s.

At Athol Street, Scotland Road veers off a little to the right and from this point northward is the lengthy Stanley Road, which runs through Kirkdale into Bootle. Stanley Road was laid out by Lord Derby in 1862, hence its name. The Stanley family, created the Earls of Derby, have had an association with the Liverpool vicinity for nearly a thousand years. The Earls of Derby owned huge areas of land including most of Bootle, Kirkdale and Walton besides land in other parts of the country. As a result, many local pubs are named Stanley or Derby.

23 pubs were/are on Stanley Road, (20 in Liverpool, 3 in Bootle) including the following:

West Side

Clifford Arms

The first pub on Stanley Road was the Clifford Arms, standing on the corner of Athol Street. In this photograph from 1905, the adjoining shop was listed to Thomas Gannaway, tobacconist. By the 1950s, it was still owned by the same family and listed to Mrs Edith Gannaway. It is currently a different business.
This site housed one of the first pubs of this vicinity, listed in the 1820s, at the junction of Athol Street and Gore Street North and named the Paul Clifford Tavern. At that time, Gore Street North was only a narrow track as far as Rake Lane and the pub was surrounded by countryside. By the 1860s, as the ever expanding town engulfed the rural vicinity, Gore Street North was swallowed up by Stanley Road, which was built up well beyond Rake Lane, by the renamed Latham Street. The pub was still named the Paul Clifford Tavern in the 1850s (then at 259 Athol Street). After the 1860s (probably rebuilt in this period), its name was shortened to its present one and, after numerical changes, adopted the current address. The premises are currently closed.

Cunard Hotel

Open to date, on the corner of Stanley Road and Boundary Street. This photograph is from approximately 1960, when the pub was a Bents House and the manager was Peter Joseph Lamb. At this time, demolition was in progress around the pub which currently stands in isolation.

Police Report 1892: 'This house has a dancing license, and is frequented by young persons of both sexes, who, after the dancing ceases about 10.30 pm, retire to the business part of the house, where they remain until 11 pm.'

Evelyn House

Situated on the corner of Stanley Road and Evelyn Street, this pub was known locally as Mary Reagans, a former manageress. Listed 1970.

Mediterranean

These premises listed at 119a Stanley Road and 101 Latham Street, were known locally as Kittys. This view is from 1908, when the pub was managed by Michael Brosnan. Listed 1970. This site is now open land.

Police Report 1892: 'Permitting drunkenness, dismissed'.

Admiralty

Located at the junction of Stanley Road and Aspinall Street, this pub was named the Admiral when first listed in the 1860s, then, somewhat strangely, its name changed to the Cat during the 1890s. By 1898, it was called the Admiral Hotel until it took its final name in the early 1960s, when this photograph was taken. It retained its nickname of the Cat until demolition in the 1970's. Police Report 1900: 'Selling drink to a drunken man. Bound over'.

Blackledge's shop was on the other junction of Aspinall Street, whilst the shops on the adjoining block in the 1960s were:

153   E.R. Hughes and Sons Ltd., butchers
155   Mrs Mary Catherine Mullen, ladies hairdressers
157   Mrs Mary Bolger, baker
159   Pat Burns, general dealer
161   Mrs Delaney, dry cleaners
163   Mr Richard (Dick) Curtin, grocer
165   Francis Hill, Chemist

Lighthouse

These premises, on the corner of Stanley Road and Lambeth Road, have opened and closed a number of times of late and are currently open and standing in isolation. When photographed in approximately 1960, the manager was Percy Thomas.
The adjoining shops were:

173   William Ross, greengrocer
175   Len Heaton, men's outfitters
177   Simister Bros., fishmongers
179   S. Grodner, draper
181   not listed
183   James Mitty Ltd, tripe dresser
185   Roy Quinn Ltd, grocers

Stanley Arms

Modern houses now occupy this site at the junction of Stanley Road and Elstow Street. Quite a crowd watched when this photograph was taken in 1908, when the manager was George Tomlinson. Listed 1964.

Knowsley Hotel

Open to date and aptly named for the vicinity, as explained earlier, the Knowsley Hotel is known locally as the Round House. Listed at 329 at the junction with Commercial Road. When this photograph was taken in the 1920s, the manager was Matthew Fitzsimons. The pub is also known locally as Billy Brooks, a former manager.

Stanley Arms

Listed at 451 Stanley Road and 1 Wolsey Street and situated just before the Bootle boundary. Photographed in the 1920s, when the manager was Alfred John Fishlock, this was an excellent example of a flamboyant Victorian PH. Its replacement, a typical 1960s structure now named the Pitch Pine, cannot be compared architecturally to its predecessor.

Police Report 1903: 'Back door opens into enclosed sub-let stable yard, the gate of which opens into Wolsey ßtreet. The gate when closed prevents the police having access to the rear of the premises.'

The three shops in this photograph were:

449   Mrs Clara Smith, tobacconist and stationer.

447   E. and A.C. Cudmore, ladies outfitters.

445   Hugh McCann, fried fish dealer.

The following is in Bootle, where numbering changes:

Swifts

Open to date at 31/33 Stanley Road and Viola Street and originally the aptly named Derby Arms. In common with the modern trend, its new name was taken from a former manager, Thomas Swift, who managed the pub in the 1920s (when photographed).

The two shops on this view were at 33, Inch and Lister, pork butchers (at one time part of the pub) and at 35, Samuel J. Liggett, grocers and provision dealers (to date a licensed betting office).

Grapes Hotel

On the eastside of Stanley Road, the Grapes Hotel stood at the junction of Stanley Road and Boundary Street. Prior to its demolition in the 1980s, it was known locally as Smokin' Joes. The site is currently derelict land. The Georgian housing on Boundary Street, despite having listed status, was demolished in 1994, partly because of long time neglect.

Grapes

During the 1960s, this pub, on the corner of Stanley Road and Latham Street, was known locally as Pat Malloys. Pat was the manager and his two brothers, Jimmy and Tommy, were renowned Liverpool boxers during the 1940s and 1950s. Jimmy was one of the best welterweights that Liverpool ever produced yet he never won the title that his ability deserved. His only title chance came near the end of his career when he met the then unbeaten rising star, Wally Thom of Birkenhead, in 1950. Wally took the newly instituted Central Area Title. However, Jimmy got his revenge in the following year by beating Thom in two rounds on a cut eye stoppage. When his professional career (which lasted from 1939 to 1952) ended, Jimmy went on to manage his younger brother. Tommy is one of the few fighters who can claim the distinction of winning a British title ,with an unbeaten record. In July 1958, he beat Jimmy Newman (Walthamstow) on points over 15 gruelling rounds at Streatham Ice Rink, London, and lifted the vacant welter title.

The pub itself is now the site of a police station. When this photograph was taken in the 1920s, the licensee was Mary Hawley. Listed 1970.

Although Stanley Road starts at Athol Street, Scotland Road veers off at this junction a little northward, were it finally ends at Boundary Street. From here its continuation is Kirkdale Road where the following were/are, from originally 17 pubs:

replace the terraced property has also been demolished. The former shops on Kirkdale Road have also been replaced by housing that is still standing.

Police Report 1892: 'Domino playing allowed in this house'.

Mersey Hotels

This pub, at the corner of Kirkdale Road and Great Mersey Street, displayed a Walker's sign when photographed in 1905, while on the window was written 'Joules Stone Ales' (see Neptune, Great Howard Street). The pub was managed at this time by Thomas Lindsay. Note the men's toilet outside the premises. The premises was demolished in the 1970s and the site has since been replaced by landscaping. The adjoining premises on Kirkdale Road were listed as Cocoa Rooms.

Hamlet Hotel

Open to date at 1 Kirkdale Road and 249 Boundary Street. The photograph is from the 1950s, when the pub was a Threlfall's house and managed by William Thomas Owens. In the 1830s, a pub named the Golden Lion was listed at this site (then 2 Boundary Street). By 1848, it was listed at 1-3 Kirkdale Road and 2 Boundary Street. In 1855, it was managed by Alice Gradwell and, by 1859, numerical changes had occurred and the premises was listed at their present address. This was the last year that the name, Golden Lion, exists. After this, the pub was called the Hamlet Hotel.

Police report 1903: 'Selling drink to a drunken man. Dismissed'.

Crown Vaults

The Crown Vaults are presently standing vacant at the junction of Kirkdale Road and Wrexham Street. The terraced housing of Wrexham Street has been demolished and, typical of so many housing schemes since the 1960s, the housing that was built to

Goats Head

This highly decorative, former Higson's pub was listed at 63 to 67 Kirkdale Road at its junction with Smith Street and photographed in the late 1970s. The site is currently open land. Listed 1970.

Alexandra

This large pub occupied the corner of Kirkdale Road and Whittle Street. The adjoining shops were empty and awaiting demolition when photographed in the 1970s. The site of the pub and shops has since been replaced by landscaping. Whittle Street still remains.

Liver Hotel

Listed at 149-151 Kirkdale Road at its junction with Morley Lane and displaying a Liver Bird. These premises, possibly of ancient date, were listed in the 1820s and probably existed before Kirkdale Road was named (when it was part of the old road to Ormskirk). The last Public Act of the seventeenth century connected with Liverpool, was the constitution of the borough into a separate parish from Walton in 1699. A Bill was brought into Parliament exhibiting the reasons for the proposed change. A portion of the Bill is as follows:

'And there being but one chapel, which doth not contain one-half of our inhabitants in the Summer, upon pretence of going to the parish church, which is two long miles, and there being a village in the way, they drink in the said village, by which and otherwise many youth and sundry families are ruined: therefore it is hoped the bill may pass, being to promote the service of God'. The village was Kirkdale and this pub, located at the edge of the old village, may well have been the one mentioned in the Bill. When photographed in the 1920s, the manager was John William Capstick. An adjoining bakery was listed to W Hankin. The site of the pub and Morley Lane are now part of the surrounds of an enclosed football pitch. Listed 1970.

Pembroke Castle

Listed at 163 Kirkdale Road and photographed in 1912, when the pub was managed by James Molyneaux. The site is grassland surrounding the previously mentioned football pitch. Not listed 1940s.

The following three, from originally five were on Latham Street (originally Rake Lane).

Lathom House Hotel

Listed at 1 Latham Street at its junction with Commercial Road. Photographed in the 1960s, when the pub had ceased trading and was in use as a betting shop. Note the spelling of the pub as Lathom, whilst the street was Latham. The name Lathom commemorates a family who owned Knowsley (which used to be one of the largest single estates in the country) since the 12th century. Through the marriage, in 1385, of Sir John De Stanley to Isabella de Lathom, Knowsley and Lathom became the chief seats of the family.

Sefton Arms

This pub stood on the corner of Latham Street and Vesuvius Street (abolished). When photographed in approximately 1908, the manager was Thomas Parry. The premises closed in the 1920s and was later in use as a snooker hall. Modern houses now occupy this site.

Police Report 1903: 'March, selling drink to a drunken man. 20/- and costs. April, selling drink to a drunken man. 40/- and costs'.

Queens Arms Hotel

This pub, which stood at the corner of Latham Street and Smith Street, extended along Latham Street to the junction of Bewley Street. When photographed in the 1960s, the manager was Thomas Ward. The building shown behind the pub, between Back Bewley Street and Pluto Street, was a pub called the Grapes. Both were listed in 1964. Modern housing now occupies the former streets. Before the 1860s, the premises was named Orrells Vaults and were listed at 376 Rake Lane. The owner was John Orrell who, together with his brother Joseph, had a brewery in Wrexham Street some 200 yards away (the premises appear to have originally been a private house, before additions). John Orrell had a house built in Anfield Road which had a field behind it that extended to Walton Breck Road. The land adjoining this field belonged to his brother Joseph and was partly owned by John Houlding and was still undeveloped in the 1880s. Everton FC acquired this land in 1884, developing it as a football ground, Anfield. By the 1890s, after Everton moved to Goodison Park, Anfield became the home of Liverpool FC. (Incidentally, part of John Orrell's former home is now the site of the Shankly Gates outside the ground).

Britannia Hotel

The Brittannia Hotel was one of originally 4 pubs in Smith Street and was listed at its junction with Great Mersey Street. In this photograph from the late 1950s, advertising for 'Ind Coope's Double Diamond' and 'Allsopp's Special Stout' can be seen. The manager at this time was Thomas Kinsella. Listed 1970. A modern building now stands on the site.

In the 1860's, immense changes were about to take place as the whole area was engulfed by terraced streets and the old Kirkdale village was wiped off the map. The tenements in Whittle Street, shown above photographed in 1902 is of a type of housing that has now vanished from Liverpool. It is hard to imagine nowadays, that this type of property was a huge improvement on previous living conditions. The first municipal tenements in the city, in fact the first in the country, were erected in 1869 in Silvester Street and called St Martin's Cottages. Sadly, these were demolished in the 1970s. The tenements in this street were also cleared in the 1970s.

Harcourt Hotel

A Threlfall's pub, listed at 36 to 38 Harcourt Street at its junction with Chelmsford Street, off Lambeth Road. Frederick Whewell managed the pub during the early 1970s when photographed. The site was replaced with housing in the 1970s.

Westminster Road, originally Bootle Lane, as its old name indicates, was an old highway leading from Kirkdale to Bootle. It is still a major road today, although many of the numerous former side streets have been cleared. A scattering of pubs remain on the road from an original total of 12, including the following.

Claremont

Listed at 93 Westminster Road at its junction with a narrow alley named Grove Place. This photograph is from the early 1960s, when the Claremont was managed by Margaret Ellen Towers. The adjoining chemist was listed to Rae Hartley. Listed 1970. The site later became part of a school play ground.

Queens Arms

Photographed in 1912, the Queens Arms (opposite bottom right) was listed at 63 to 65 Westminster Road. Modern housing now stands on the site. The pub was known as the Bath House due to its location close to Westminster Road swimming baths.

Half Way House

Listed at the corner of Westminster Road and Whitefield Lane, the Half Way House was demolished along with the surrounding property and Whitefield Lane during the 1970s. The site is now part of a housing estate. The manageress of the pub, when photographed in the early 1970s, was Annie Agnes Fellows.

Westminster Hotel

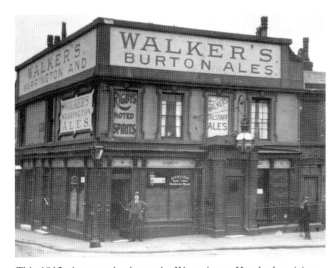

This 1912 photograph, shows the Westminster Hotel advertising Walker's and Rigby's Ales. At the corner of Westminster Road and Kirkstall Street, modern housing now occupies this site.

Sefton Arms

Open to date on the corner of Westminster Road and Bradewell Street (originally Margaret Street), Little change has been made to the exterior of the pub. The shop on the left was a confectioner's belonging to Wilfred Latham and is currently a newsagent. The pub is known locally as Banjo Bennetts.

Westminster

Open to date at 214 Westminster Road. The houses on the right were demolished in the 1960s. Two once common sights can be seen: a street tap and a horse trough. The premises are currently named the Grand National. The pub was known locally as the Minneries.

Grapes Inn

Listed at 17 Sellar Street (originally King Street) at its junction with Summer Gardens, off Westminster Road. This view from approximately 1960, shows Westminster Road swimming baths. Although the baths remain to date, the frontage shown here has since been demolished. The pub was kown as Ivy Sloans.

BH

Barlow Lane veers off north easterly towards Spellow Lane. This former Threlfalls BH was one of two pubs that were listed at Barlow Lane at its junction with Netley Street. Photographed in the 1930s, modern housing now occupies this site.

Barlow Hotel

Open to date at 62Barlow Street, behind Westminster Road and almost facing the Westminster PH. This pub shows little exterior difference from when it was photographed in the 1920s. The premises are known locally as the Dark House.

The following is in Bankhall (a district of Kirkdale which, even now, is often mistaken as being in Bootle) which is an ancient settlement. The Moore family, originally residing at Old Hall, Old Hall Street, Liverpool, moved to a new residence in Kirkdale in about 1280. They named it Bank Hall, hence the district's name. The building stood for nearly 500 years until demolition in the late 1770s.

Miranda Hotel

This small corner local is open to date. Listed at 39 Miranda Road and 39 Celia Street, this view is from the 1920s, when the manager was Henry Wilson. Adverts for 'Christmas Ales' can be seen on the windows. The premises are currently standing in isolation. The photograph above shows the Miranda football team, Liverpool and District Alliance League Champions Division 1 1931 to 32.

Police Report 1902: 'Allowing riotous behaviour on the premises. Dismissed'.

Returning to Kirkdale Road, its continuation at Everton Valley is Walton Road where the following were/are, from originally 17:

Tintern Abbey

This pub, listed at 103 Walton Road and 69 Tintern Street, was only closed and demolished in the 1980s. The adjoining shops were empty and awaiting demolition when photographed in approximately 1980. The site is now landscaped.

Netley

Still trading at the junction of Walton Road and Langham Street, this view is from 1912, when Phipps's Netley Hotel was displayed on a board on the side of the premises. The adjoining shop was listed to John Cosletts, butcher and is currently a different business.

Palatine

Listed at the corner of Walton Road and Barlow Lane, this pub ceased trading in the early 1930s and was replaced by the present building in 1935. The site then became a shop, Burton Men's Outfitters and has recently changed to a different business. Photographed in the 1920s, when the manager was Louis Joseph Henshell.

The following concerns the Clock, which is still open at 167 Walton Road. Shortly after the pub was built in 1875, an application for a licence for the premises was made by John Boyd at the Kirkdale Quarter Sessions. Through his solicitor, he applied for a transfer of his own licence from 26 Lawrence Road, off Scotland Road. because his own premises was required to be pulled down under the Provisions of the Artisans Dwelling Act. The court was told that the property to be pulled down comprised of four acres and was amongst the worst class of court property in Liverpool. Despite everything being in order, a licence was refused on the grounds that the court was only entitled to consider the removal of a licence of a public house from one part of a licensed district to another part of the same district.

There were regular changes at that time concerning licensing

laws, including the following two: 'That on weekdays, licensed houses in England outside the metropolis should not be open before 7 am, and that they should be closed one hour earlier than at present on week days. That on Sundays licensed houses in the metropolis should be opened from one to three pm for consumption off the premises only, and for consumption on the premises from 7 to 11 pm that in other places in England they should be open from 12 30 to 2 30 pm for consumption off the premises only, and for consumption on the premises from 7 to 10 pm in populous places, and from 7 to 9 pm in others'. This was one of the reasons that so many pubs existed in the older parts of the town. This particular case could have been pursued by Mr Boyd, through a different section of a licensing act of 1872, but it was apparently not followed through.

Derby Arms

This large, flamboyant pub (opposite top) at 2 Walton Road at its junction with Everton Valley, had carved, glazed pillars on its frontage. The Lyric Super Cinema can be seen in the background of this 1920's photograph. This was only a cinema between 1922 and 1925, prior to this it was a theatre (the Lyric). In 1925, it reopened as a theatre once again, only to close down in 1932.

Before the pub's demolition in the early 1980s, the stage door of the old theatre could still be seen. Road improvements were the feeble excuse for the demolition of this magnificent structure. Police Report 1892: 'The licensee does not appear to take any part in the management of the business'. The registered owner in that year was named as the Earl of Derby, Knowsley Hall.

Bronte

The Bronte stood on the corner of Walton Lane and Royal Street and was named after a former house, Bronte House and estate that occupied land close to the pub. This has since been covered by terraced property between Walton Lane and Sleepers Hill. Photographed in the 1970s. The premises was demolished in the 1980s as part of a scheme for road improvements.

Springfield House

This excellent view shows an ancient windmill in Springfield Square, off Walton Road in 1919. It has long since been demolished, together with the housing of the Square, although the PH shown partly on the left, the Springfield House, remains open to date. Listed at 232 Walton Road.

Woodhouse

The Woodhouse stood at the junction of Walton Lane and Woodhouse Street and was demolished during the 1970s with the site now part of a widened Walton Lane. Woodhouse Street and Bronte Street, Liverpool 3, were also named after Bronte House. This view is from the 1950s and the shops that can be seen were:

35   Ladies hairdresser listed to Mrs Hilda McKibbin

33   Tory Laundry (Liverpool) Ltd

31   Photographer listed to Joseph Green

29   Chandler listed to Mrs Catherine Linder

27   Milk bar listed to A Duor

Britannia

The Britannia stood at the junction of Walton Lane and Florence Street and was demolished in the 1970s for road improvements. Landscaping has replaced this pub. This photograph is from the 1920s.

Abbey

The Abbey, at the junction of Walton Lane and Tetlow Street, is one of only two pubs left on Walton Lane. In the 1870s and 1880s, these premises was named the Atlantic Hotel. In the early 1870s, they were named the Park Hotel and in the 1860s, McNaught's Hotel. The early view is from the 1890s and the second view is from the 1920s. Extensive alterations include a new storey similar to today. The old marker outside the pub still remains and reads: 'Borough of Liverpool Town Hall 2 miles 826 yards, height above old dock sill 145.5'.

Walton on the Hill is an ancient settlement which had Liverpool under its ecclesiastical jurisdiction until 1699. In common with all ancient settlements, the community was located around the parish church, St Mary's. Originally the parish church of Liverpool, the church is more commonly referred to as Walton Church. Somewhat unusually, the church is not located in the centre of the old village but on its edge. In the rural pre-1850s, the settlement extended along the present Walton village and some way along Cherry Lane. Together with most ancient churches, rebuilding and additions have occurred over the years. Founded in 1326 (on the site of an earlier church), the main body was rebuilt in 1742. Additions include the chancel (1810) and the west tower (1828-32). Sadly, the church suffered extensive war damage, although rebuilt by 1953 to a very high standard.

The following is from the annals of 1854: 'The original font is preserved near the centre of the church yard, having been removed hither some years ago from a public house door, where it had long lain desecrated'. The pub was apparently the Brown Cow and the font was in use as an aid for mounting horses.

The following 2 are in County Road, from 6 pubs: (originally part of Rice Lane).

A row of landing houses on Walton Lane, with a slight view of
the Abbey when photographed in the early 1960s. These houses
have since been demolished, leaving the pub isolated.

Black Horse

Listed at 284 County Road and photographed in 1973. This site,
adjacent to Walton Church, has housed an inn for centuries. The
present pub now serves a much more densely populated Walton.

One of the pubs of County Road, at number 143 and open to
date, is the County Hotel. The site of this pub housed an ancient
inn, close to a toll bar in the 19th century. The regulars of today
luckily do not have to drink with the regulars of some 150 years
ago, as the following article from 1888 explains: 'A toll-gate
stood near Stuart Road till removed fifteen years since, although
it had ceased to be used as a spot for levying tolls for about ten
years previously. Near the toll bar on the site of the County
Hotel, corner of Stuart Road and County Road, stood a small inn,
where the weary traveller might get refreshments and where, in
the days of body snatching, within the last fifty years, many of
those nefarious traders stopped to drink'.

Harlech Castle

Open to date at 63 County Road at its junction with Newark Street, the Harlech Castle is a typical late 19th century building with fine details.

Spellow House

Spellow House is open to date at 79 Goodison Road. Its name is taken from the ancient Spellowe House built about 1270 in the vicinity. When the familiar terraced streets were built in the late 19th century, many were named after the Welsh builders responsible for their construction. However Goodison Road is not Welsh and its name is synonymous with Everton Football Club who opened the first purpose built stadium in the country here in 1892. The name Goodison is thought to have come from a civil engineer George William Goodison, although a Mr Goodison and Son was listed as licensee of the Derby in nearby Walton Road in the 1850s.

Beehive

The Beehive is probably of ancient date and was listed at 2 Smithy Lane (abolished) at its junction with Church Lane, close to Walton Church. The premises closed in the 1920s. The man in this view from 1905 was probably the manager, Joseph Bennett posing with his family. (Note what appears to be a beehive displayed over the door).

Hill House

These premises, listed at 40 Breeze Hill, at the junction with Peveril Street, were demolished as part of the scheme for the Rice Lane flyover. When photographed in the 1920s, the manager was John Thomas Evans.

The following were/are on Rice Lane, from a total of 9 pubs. Rice Lane was named after the former Rice family who had a house and land hereabouts.

Rice House

Listed at 1 Rice Lane and located at the junction of Breeze Hill, adjacent to Walton Town Hall. Demolished to make way for the Rice Lane flyover,

Prince Leopold

Open to date at the corner of Rice Lane and Rawcliffe Street, this pub shows little exterior difference from this 1920s view. Royal names predominant on Rice Lane with pubs named after Queen Victoria (1819-1901) and her 4 sons:

57	Queen Victoria.
155/157	Prince Of Wales: A title conferred upon eldest son and heir apparent (Edward VII -1901-1910).
265/267	Prince Alfred (second son).
92	Prince Arthur (third son).
185	Prince Leopold (fourth son).

Queen Victoria also had 5 daughters. (Queen Victoria's consort, Prince Albert, is commemorated in the nearby County Road, although it has recently adapted its former nickname - the Red Brick). Nowadays, royal names are not adopted as they were in the past and the Prince Of Wales has recently changed names to the Beer Engine, although it will still presumably be called the Sod House by regulars (a name apparently originating from when sods were used as coolants in the cellar).

Prince Alfred

Still trading to date at 265 Rice Lane.

Stanley

This former Higson's house was listed at 142 Rice Lane, facing Walton Hospital. The alley next to the pub was named Stanley Yard and led to another alley named Throstle's Nest. The premises was demolished in the 1980s and a large supermarket has recently opened on adjacent land.

Brown Cow

Listed at 2 Rice Lane, at the side of Walton Church, and, like the Black Horse at the other side of the church, is of ancient date. The first view is from the 1890s, when the manager's name was clearly displayed as H. Guy (Henry) along with a picture of a brown cow. The premises was demolished and replaced by a highly decorated pub, early this century which had an inscription 'Ye Olde Brown Cow' on its facade, perhaps to make people believe it was the original! Sadly this pub and all the surrounding property, including Walton Town Hall were demolished in the 1960s, when the Rice Lane fly-over was constructed.

Queen Anne

The Queen Anne is still trading at 20 Fazakerley Road, off Rice Lane.

Black Bull Inn

Located in Black Bull Place between Warbreck Moor and Longmoor Lane. In the last century, the Black Bull Inn was located out in the country, on the edge of the ancient Warbreck Moor (after which the road was named). The view from the 1880s, shows the name Hall's Black Bull Inn (after John Hall) displayed on the facade. The exterior of the present structure is still the same as the view from the 1930s.

Sefton Arms Hotel

Listed at 2 Ormskirk Road, this huge PH was also photographed in the 1920s when racing was in progress. A modern pub of the same name now occupies this site.

Queens Arms

Listed at 240 Warbreck Moor and located close to the Sefton Arms Hotel, This view from the 1920s, shows crowds of people gathered around, presumably because racing was in progress at the nearby Aintree Racecourse. A subsequent pub of the same name, which is open to date, has replaced this building.

Windsor Castle

Another royal connection, the Windsor Castle was located at the junction of Orrell Lane and Walton Vale. Photographed in 1908, when the manager was John Redfearn. A date of 1880 is displayed. The premises was destroyed during the War and its replacement is now named the Windsor.

Farmers Arms

Listed at 212 Longmoor Lane, this view of the Farmers Arms was taken before the First World War. The premises was closed and demolished in 1961, the year that the present building was built, set back a little from the line of the road. The last manager of the original pub and first of the new one, was George Alcock.

Railway

Listed at 273 Longmoor Lane. Written on the gable end, when photographed in the 1920s, is 'Ellis Warde and Co's Noted Ales'. This Brewery was registered in 1897 in Ormskirk, Lancashire and was taken over by Walker Cain in 1929, with 102 licensed houses. The Railway was demolished in 1967, when the licensee was Harry Hogg, and replaced by the Chaser, which is set back from the road.

The following two are located in the suburb of Aintree:

Blue Anchor

Located in School Lane and listed in 1815 as the Anchor, this pub was probably built during the late 18th century in connection with the Leeds – Liverpool canal. The following is from an 1871 census: 'John Poe, unmarried, aged 41, publican and farmer of 10 statute acres, employing one boy and brother (surveyor of highways), sister, two cousins, servant'. The premises was named the Blue Anchor by the 1880s. These views are from 1909. The present building, which bears the same name, is a more recent building.

Old Roan

Open to date in Copy Lane, the Old Roan is another inn of possible ancient date. The view from 1904, shows the pub when it belonged to Thorougood's Brewery. The premises was 'out in the country' until comparatively recently. Its replacement has recently adopted a typical 1990s name, the Tut 'n Shive. The following is from an 1861 census concerning this pub: 'Richard Meadows, aged 32, publican and farmer of 16 acres, employing two labourers, one boy and wife, four children, one step-daughter, five servants (two general, three agricultural labourers).'

Bootle Arms

The Bootle Arms is an ancient inn, that is open to date and located in Melling, just beyond Aintree (named as Melling Rocks on this view, now Rock Lane). Cromwell is supposed to have stopped off at the inn during 1643, while marching to battle at Preston. The name derives from the Bootle family, who had settled in the area centuries ago and farmed the land. Their motto is displayed outside the premises. The church St Thomas, also of ancient date, is said to have been built on an even earlier pagan burial ground. This photograph is from approximately 1906. The same view today has the church hidden by mature trees, whilst the small out-house alongside the pub has gone and the building on the right has been demolished and replaced by modern houses.

The following three were/are located in Kirkby:

Farmers Arms

Another pub of ancient date at the junction of Headbolt Lane and Pingwood Lane that served the farming community for centuries. Photographed when still open in the 1950s. At the edge of the Tower Hill estate, the site is currently landscaped.

Copplehouse

Still trading at the junction of Copplehouse Lane and Longmoor
Lane, the Copplehouse stands just beyond the Liverpool
boundary. This photograph is from the 1930s when it was a
Threlfall's house. The ornate lamp at the entrance is no longer
standing. The view of the interior was typical of the period.
Apparently, during the war an American serviceman asked for a
drink, after the towel had been put on. Upon refusal, he
demanded to know why. 'Time Sir', replied the Barman. 'What
time?' asked the American, (not realising the old licensing laws).
'That time' said the Barman pointing to the clock whereupon the
service man pulled a gun out and shot the clock off the wall.
'Can I have a drink now Sir?' was supposed to have been his
calm reply.

Carters Arms

Open to date and located in Glovers Brow, these premises appear
to have been built as a private house, although they were licensed
when photographed in the 1920s. The small out-building on this
view has since been replaced by an extension of the pub which
now has a beer garden.

Bootle

Bootle, in common with many town-ships surrounding Liverpool, was recorded in the Domesday Book, yet remained sparsely populated for centuries. Amongst the owners of the Manor of Bootle were the Moore family and the Earls Of Derby. As late as the early 19th century, the population of Bootle was little over 500. Bootle-cum-Linacre was incorporated as a borough in 1868 and Bootle in 1890. From the 1860s, the borough grew at an enormous rate as docks, warehouses, factories and the railway rapidly transformed the rural vicinity into a major industrial area.

The importance of Bootle is well recorded by the fact that the area suffered more bomb attacks for its size than any other British town during the Second World War. In 1974, the country was changed geographically with new Metropolitan Counties, including the new County of Merseyside, which incorporated Sefton (of which Bootle became a part). Prior to this, the original boroughs had their own identity (e.g. Borough of Bootle and Litherland Urban County Council, Borough of Crosby)

In the early 19th century a number of inns existed in Bootle, probably frequented by day trippers from Liverpool, who were visiting the sandy beaches of the north shore. Amongst them were: Bootle Coffee House, Black Bull, Eagle and Child and the Rimrose Hotel. All were listed in the 1820s, with the latter surviving until its destruction during the Second World War. Another inn existing well before the borough was formed was the Sun, Merton Road, renamed the Railway by the 1870s and probably rebuilt and open to date (see the Jawbone).

The following were/are in Bootle and district.

Windham Hotel

When photographed (above) in 1927, patriotism was in full bloom outside the Windham Hotel, located at the junction of Oriel Road and St Edmonds Road. The occasion was the opening of the Gladstone Dock by King George V and Queen Mary. The pub was managed during this time by Mrs Mary Littler. After a period of closure, the premises have recently reopened and are currently named Renaghans.

Clarence

The Clarence is open to date and situated on the corner of Canal Street and Bridge Street (close to the former pub). The first photograph, from 1908, when the manager was Henry Littler, shows the pub advertising 'Christmas Ales'. The second view is from the 1930s, when the rebuilt pub was still managed by Mr Littler, shows a typical interior of the times. (These Littlers were probably from the same family as the licensee of Windham Hotel).

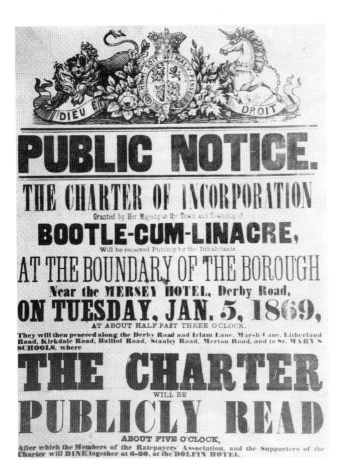

Hawthorne Hotel

Open to date on the corner of Hawthorne Road and Bedford Road, the Hawthorne Hotel is a typical late 19th century building where some detail has gone into the structure. Photographed in the 1950s, when the manager was Gerard Williams. The former grocer's shop Irwins, has since been incorporated into the pub.

Albion

Still trading at the junction of Hawthorne Road and Earl Road, this is another Threlfalls house, photographed in the 1950s. Typical of Threlfalls in the fact that the name of the pub was not displayed.

Charter

Two public houses, both in Derby Road, are named in a Charter of 1869: The Mersey Hotel, near the Liverpool boundary, and the Dolphin. The last licensee of the Dolphin, John Hudson, was refused a removal of his license in 1879. Justices of the Borough of Bootle, refused to grant him a removal of a license from the Dolphin Hotel, 126 Derby Road, to the Grove Hotel, Rimrose Road, a distance of about three quarters of a mile. A Dr Cummins stated that the appellant had kept the Dolphin Hotel for about eighteen years (before the Borough was formed). He was a yearly tenant and the London and Northwestern Railway Company, under their Act of 1874, had taken the premises which had now been taken down. No compensation had been paid to him and he could not expect to get any. The Bootle Justices refused the application made to them without giving any reason for so doing.

Hawthorne Road (originally part of Bootle Lane) and its vicinity was built up during the 19th century by a Welsh builder, William Jones who became a Liberal councillor in Bootle. He was an ardent teatotaller who refused to sell or let any of his land for use as licensed premises. Hence there are only 2 pubs on this road (obviously not on Mr Jones' land).

Royal Standard Hotel

First listed in the 1860s, at 78 Millers Bridge, this pub was originally named the Masonic. The premises, photographed in the 1920s, were demolished in the 1970s. They were known locally as Mick Healeys, after a former licensee.

Derby Arms

Open to date at the junction of Irlam Road and Strand Road, this pub has been in existence since at least the 1820s, when it was listed as the Derby Arms Hotel, Bootle Marsh. An 1841 census reveals: 'John Percival, innkeeper, aged 40 and Mary Percival aged 30 and 4 children, 4 servants.' (Also listed as coach proprietor). The photograph is from the 1920s when the manager was George Eveleigh. After a period of closure, the premises have recently reopened and are currently named JFKs Irish Bar.

Jawbone

Listed at 12 Litherland Road, the Jawbone is arguably Bootle's oldest pub. The date 1802 is displayed on the side of the premises. The following is an 1878 letter to the Bootle Times: 'The Jawbones has been very much improved and enlarged. A butchering business in a double sense was carried on by a farmer proprietor who used to supply his customers with butcher's meat as well as liquor. The butcher's shop has disappeared like the cottages adjoining the Stanley Arms and has served to make the Jawbones into a large spirit vaults'.

Note the spelling of the pub in the letter as Jawbones. This name originates from when whaling was a major industry in Liverpool during the late 18th and early 19th centuries. This trade is recalled in street names such as Greenland Street (where there was a boiling house) and Baffin Street (Baffin being the name of the last trading whaler).

The fashionable collecting of whale bones was quite common throughout Liverpool with bones being used mainly as ornaments and garden additions. This declined rapidly with the demise of the industry and, by the 1890s, practically no bones were in existence. It was during this period that a paper was written recalling some of the many sites where whale bones had simply been discarded or buried. "The old Zoological Gardens, West Derby Road, had jaw bones as an ornamental entrance inside to higher ground." "Jaw bones were set up in 1840 as an entrance to a market garden at the north corner of Fairclough Lane" (site of the Royal Liverpool Hospital).

Many bones were found buried at the south side of James Street, whilst in Breckfield Road North, near the St Domingo Pit, bones were dug up near to where they had been fixed as a garden entrance. Other sites included Boundary Lane, Whitefield Lane, Everton Brow, Swiss Road, Elm Park, Lodge Lane, Wavertree Village and Little Brighton (Crosby) When the old Waterloo Hotel in Ranleigh Street was demolished for the erection of Central Station, quite a number where found which were apparently removed to the grounds of a hotel at Hightown Station. It was ascertained that the majority of bones found were those of the Greenland Whale which grows to a length of between sixty and eighty-feet. According to the paper, there were only two bones remaining by the 1890s. One, a lower jaw bone, stood thirteen feet above the ground on a site at the top of Holt Hill. The other stood nine feet above the ground in Ibbotsons Lane, Greenbank.

Stanley Arms

Open to date at 74 Litherland Road, the premises are shown in 1912, when the licensee was John Carden. They have since altered significantly from this view. The cottages shown to the left have been demolished. The living accommodation in the centre remains, whilst the frontage of the pub was rebuilt in 1985 and extends past the smaller section of the house. The warehouse in the background, part of a former tannery, still remains, although the two tall chimneys have been demolished.

Bridge Inn

The Bridge Inn was listed at 110 Litherland Road. Photographed in 1908, when the manager was Thomas Henry Jones (probably the man standing at the door). First licensed in about 1868, the premises have been rebuilt since this early photograph and recently the pub was renamed King Dicks (its current name).

Linacre

Listed at 46 Linacre Lane and standing in isolation, the Linacre could dispute the Jawbone as Bootle's oldest pub. Strangely, in a directory of 1878, there is no mention of any victualler in Linacre Lane yet, in an application for a licence in 1903, it was stated that the house had long been licensed to sell beer prior to 1869. It also said that the premises was rebuilt in 1888. In photographing the cellar of the pub, I discovered another cellar below the cellar in use, probably the cellar of the original premises when the pub was at a lower level than the present. The building was then named the Horse and Jockey. The original pub was probably built when the nearby Leeds – Liverpool canal was constructed in the late 18th century. Adjoining the pub, during the early years of the 20th century, was a foundry employing some 80 men and a rope works that employed some 70 men.

Alexandra Hotel

Listed at the corner of Marsh Lane and Audley Street, this former Threlfall's house was managed by Thomas Drury when photographed in the 1950s. The pub and street, along with a number of other streets in the vicinity, were demolished in the 1960s. A modern pub of the same name now stands close to the original site.

St George's Tavern

Listed at 238 Marsh Lane, the premises still display the picture of St George as featured on this view from the 1920s. A feature of this pub is an exquisite stained glass ceiling depicting St George's legendary fight with the dragon. The pub is currently closed.

Grove Hotel

Listed at 145 Rimrose Road at its junction with Grove Street, the Grove Hotel was one of originally four pubs. Rimrose Road is the continuation of Derby Road and, like the former, was badly destroyed during the war, hence so little old property along the frontage. Photographed in the 1920s, when the manager (from 1923 to 1931) was James Francis Johnson. This pub was destroyed in the war and a housing estate, built west of the pub in the 1950s, has recently been cleared.

The following were/are in Litherland, all Liverpool 21:

Hen and Chickens

Listed at 18 Field Lane and displaying 'Blezard's Noted Ales' (the registered owner) when photographed in 1908. The licensee at this time was Margaret Jones. The license of the pub was surrendered in the 1930s for a new pub, the Jubilee Inn, Appleton Road, off Field Lane.

Pacific

One of originally four pubs, the Pacific is open to date and listed at 168 Linacre Road. The demolition of part of an adjoining factory, in the early 1990s, revealed an old Threlfalls advertisement. Another Linacre Road pub is the Salt Box, so named since the early 1990s, prior to it being the pub's nickname when named the Catherine Hotel, for some 100 years. I wonder how many locals know that the current name was in fact an earlier name of the pub pre-1890?

The following were/are in Seaforth Road: (although in Liverpool 21, this road is in Crosby)

Seaforth Hotel

The view at the top of the page is from 1958. On the left are the sheds of Seaforth and Litherland railway station. Behind are Bootle gas works and, centre/back, Johnson's Dyeworks. The pub is centre/right, at the junction of School Lane. A former bank

is at the other junction. In the forefront, are railway sidings and a scrap-yard. The scrap yard and low level railway line have gone and are now part of a modern car park and cut to Princes Way. The site of the pub is now a scrap yard. The bank (currently closed) and remainder of the block still stands, whilst the gasworks tall chimneys have gone and Johnson's Dye Works have been considerably reduced in height.

Seaforth Arms

The Seaforth Arms was listed at 12 Seaforth Road. In the 1970s, this area of Seaforth changed dramatically when a new road, Princes Way, was laid out as a route to Seaforth Dock, cutting through communities and streets. Photographed in 1905, the pub closed in the 1920s. The building became a chemist and is currently trading as a domestic appliance shop.
In 1920, the Stella cinema was built where the road curves. It closed in 1958 and is now the entrance to modern shops. The buildings on the left still remain. After the pub's closure, 26-30 Seaforth Road opened as a pub of the same name and remains open to date.

Caradoc

Still trading at the junction of Seaforth Road and Crosby Road South, the premises are pictured in approximately 1908 when a Threlfall's House and managed by Norminton George Vernon. The name of this pub and the nearby St Winifred, are derived from an ancient Welsh legend. The following extract is taken from a leaflet published by Delyn Leisure Services regarding the legend of The Holy Well of St Winefride:

'In 660 AD when Holywell (Trefynnon) was only a cluster of huts centred around a church, Winefride, the daughter of a local prince, was martyred. A timid young woman and a virgin, she was pursued by Caradoc, the son of a prince. In her fear, Winefride ran for the safety of the church but was soon caught by the enraged Caradoc who, in his anger, beheaded her. A spring rose up from where her severed head came to rest. Legend tells of Winefride's uncle, St Beuno, placing her severed head next to her body and praying that she may be whole again. Saint Winefride then rose to her feet, a white scar encircled her neck as witness to her martyrdom. Caradoc sank into the ground and was never seen again. Winefride became a nun and was made abbess of a convent at Gwytherin near Llanrwst. She died there fifteen years later and was buried in the local churchyard. Her relics were removed to Shrewsbury Abbey in 1138'.

The location of the Caradoc, facing the huge Seaforth dock is in complete contrast to years ago, when it faced Seaforth sands and was a popular destination for day trippers, particularly when the Overhead Railway was operational. During the War, the pub was a social centre for both the Merchant and Royal Navy. The pub was picked out by the British traitor, William Joyce, alias Lord Haw Haw, during his infamous propaganda talks. 'I can get any information I want from the Caradoc', he told unconvinced listeners. The premises currently stand in isolation and the dairy shown in this view has been demolished.

Red Lion

Listed at 121 Bridge Road, close to the canal, this pub is known to have been in existence since at least 1799, when it was named the White Lion. In approximately 1821, it was renamed the Red Lion. The early view is from 1904, shortly before the premises was demolished to make way for the present building.

The second photograph shows the much larger replacement shortly after the previous pub was demolished. Photographed in approximately 1908, the exterior remains similar to date.

Liverpool Arms

A typical countryside inn, listed at 77 Gorsey Lane, in the Ford district of Litherland. This photograph (opposite top) is from 1904, when the lessee was Robert Bleizard and the owner the Earl of Sefton. The pub was managed by Thomas Jones for many years and it is still referred to as Tom Jones. An 1861 census of the premises reveals the following: 'Anastasia A. Butler, widow aged 55, beer retailer born Wexford, Ireland and 3 children (barmaid, dressmaker, painter). The 1957 view (opposite below) shows the present pub being built to the side of the old pub.

White House

This pub was located just over the canal from the Red Lion and, like the former, was probably built for the passing trade on the canal. The brewer's name is clearly displayed on this view from approximately 1908, when the manager was Henry Lightfoot. The site is currently grassland. Close to here, at the junction of Church Road and Hawthorne Road, a pub named after the original was built in the 1930s and is still trading to date.

A Pub On Every Corner:

The final two volumes in this series cover Scotland Road, Everton and West Derby. Scotland Road, in particular, had an incredible number of pubs, from the most basic beer houses to flamboyant 'gin palaces'. The numerous drinking houses of Great Homer Street, Netherfield Road and other well-known thoroughfares contrast with the back-street inns hidden amongst some of the worst slum housing in Britain. Pubs have played an important role in the social history of Liverpool and the final volumes underline their significance to the lives of the local communities.